Karl Marx

A Biography

Compiled by

Karyn Lavender

Scribbles

Year of Publication 2018

ISBN : 9789352979615

Book Published by

Scribbles

(An Imprint of Alpha Editions)

email - alphaedis@gmail.com

Produced by: PediaPress GmbH

Limburg an der Lahn

Germany

http://pediapress.com/

Contents

Karl Marx

Karl Marx	
FRSA[1]	

Karl Marx in 1875

Born	5 May 1818 Trier, Grand Duchy of the Lower Rhine, Kingdom of Prussia
Died	14 March 1883 (aged 64) London, England, United Kingdom
Resting place	Tomb of Karl Marx, Highgate Cemetery, London, England, United Kingdom
Residence	Germany, France, Belgium, United Kingdom
Nationality	Stateless after 1845
Spouse(s)	
Children	7, including Jenny, Laura, and Eleanor
Parents	• Heinrich Marx (father) • Henriette Pressburg (mother)
Relatives	• Louise Juta (sister) • Jean Longuet (grandson)
Philosophy career	
Alma mater	• University of Bonn • University of Berlin • University of Jena (Ph.D.)[2]
Era	19th-century philosophy
Region	Western philosophy
School	• Continental philosophy • Marxism • Correspondence theory of truth[3]

Main interests	Politics, economics, philosophy, history
Notable ideas	Marxist terminology, surplus value, contributions to the labour theory of value, class struggle, alienation and exploitation of the worker, materialist conception of history
Signature	

Karl Marx[4] (German: [maʁks]; 5 May 1818 – 14 March 1883) was a German philosopher, economist, historian, political theorist, sociologist, journalist and revolutionary socialist.

Born in Trier to a middle-class family, Marx studied law and Hegelian philosophy. Due to his political publications, Marx became stateless and lived in exile in London, where he continued to develop his thought in collaboration with German thinker Friedrich Engels and publish his writings, researching in the reading room of the British Museum. His best-known titles are the 1848 pamphlet, *The Communist Manifesto*, and the three-volume *Das Kapital*. His political and philosophical thought had enormous influence on subsequent intellectual, economic and political history and his name has been used as an adjective, a noun and a school of social theory.

Marx's theories about society, economics and politics—collectively understood as Marxism—hold that human societies develop through class struggle. In capitalism, this manifests itself in the conflict between the ruling classes (known as the bourgeoisie) that control the means of production and the working classes (known as the proletariat) that enable these means by selling their labour power in return for wages. Employing a critical approach known as historical materialism, Marx predicted that, like previous socio-economic systems, capitalism produced internal tensions which would lead to its self-destruction and replacement by a new system: socialism. For Marx, class antagonisms under capitalism, owing in part to its instability and crisis-prone nature, would eventuate the working class' development of class consciousness, leading to their conquest of political power and eventually the establishment of a classless, communist society constituted by a free association of producers.[5] Marx actively pressed for its implementation, arguing that the working class should carry out organised revolutionary action to topple capitalism and bring about socio-economic emancipation.

Marx has been described as one of the most influential figures in human history, and his work has been both lauded and criticised. His work in economics laid the basis for much of the current understanding of labour and its relation to capital, and subsequent economic thought.[6,7,8] Many intellectuals, labour unions, artists and political parties worldwide have been influenced by Marx's work, with many modifying or adapting his ideas. Marx is typically cited as one of the principal architects of modern social science.

Life

Childhood and early education: 1818–1836

Marx was born on 5 May 1818 to Heinrich Marx (1777–1838) and Henriette Pressburg (1788–1863). He was born at Brückengasse 664 in Trier, a town then part of the Kingdom of Prussia's Province of the Lower Rhine.[9] Marx was ethnically Jewish. His maternal grandfather was a Dutch rabbi, while his paternal line had supplied Trier's rabbis since 1723, a role taken by his grandfather Meier Halevi Marx.[10] His father, as a child known as Herschel, was the first in the line to receive a secular education and he became a lawyer and lived a relatively wealthy and middle-class existence, with his family owning a number of Moselle vineyards. Prior to his son's birth, and after the abrogation of Jewish emancipation in the Rhineland, Herschel converted from Judaism to join the state Evangelical Church of Prussia, taking on the German forename of Heinrich over the Yiddish Herschel.[11] Marx was a third cousin once removed of German Romantic poet Heinrich Heine, also born to a German Jewish family in the Rhineland, with whom he became a frequent correspondent in later life.[12]Wikipedia:Citing sources

Largely non-religious, Heinrich was a man of the Enlightenment, interested in the ideas of the philosophers Immanuel Kant and Voltaire. A classical liberal, he took part in agitation for a constitution and reforms in Prussia, then governed by an absolute monarchy.[14] In 1815, Heinrich Marx began work as an attorney and in 1819 moved his family to a ten-room property near the Porta Nigra.[15] His wife, Henriette Pressburg, was a Dutch Jewish woman from a prosperous business family that later founded the company Philips Electronics. Her sister Sophie Pressburg (1797–1854) married Lion Philips (1794–1866) and was the grandmother of both Gerard and Anton Philips and great-grandmother to Frits Philips. Lion Philips was a wealthy Dutch tobacco manufacturer and industrialist, upon whom Karl and Jenny Marx would later often come to rely for loans while they were exiled in London.[16]

Little is known of Marx's childhood.[17] The third of nine children, he became the eldest son when his brother Moritz died in 1819. Young Marx and his surviving siblings, Sophie, Hermann, Henriette, Louise, Emilie and Caroline, were baptised into the Lutheran Church in August 1824 and their mother in November 1825. Young Marx was privately educated by his father until 1830,

Figure 1: *Marx's birthplace, now Brückenstraße 10, in Trier. The family occupied two rooms on the ground floor and three on the first floor. Purchased by the Social Democratic Party of Germany in 1928, it now houses a museum devoted to him*[13]

when he entered Trier High School, whose headmaster, Hugo Wyttenbach, was a friend of his father. By employing many liberal humanists as teachers, Wyttenbach incurred the anger of the local conservative government. Subsequently, police raided the school in 1832 and discovered that literature espousing political liberalism was being distributed among the students. Considering the distribution of such material a seditious act, the authorities instituted reforms and replaced several staff during Marx's attendance.[18]

In October 1835 at the age of 17, Marx travelled to the University of Bonn wishing to study philosophy and literature, but his father insisted on law as a more practical field.[19] Due to a condition referred to as a "weak chest", Marx was excused from military duty when he turned 18. While at the University at Bonn, Marx joined the Poets' Club, a group containing political radicals that were monitored by the police.[20] Marx also joined the Trier Tavern Club drinking society (*Landsmannschaft der Treveraner*), at one point serving as club co-president.[21] Additionally, Marx was involved in certain disputes, some of which became serious: in August 1836 he took part in a duel with a member of the university's Borussian Korps.[22] Although his grades in the first term were good, they soon deteriorated, leading his father to force a transfer to the more serious and academic University of Berlin.[23]

Hegelianism and early journalism: 1836–1843

Spending summer and autumn 1836 in Trier, Marx became more serious about his studies and his life. He became engaged to Jenny von Westphalen, an educated baroness of the Prussian ruling class who had known Marx since childhood. As she had broken off her engagement with a young aristocrat to be with Marx, their relationship was socially controversial owing to the differences between their religious and class origins, but Marx befriended her father Ludwig von Westphalen (a liberal aristocrat) and later dedicated his doctoral thesis to him.[24] Seven years after their engagement, on 19 June 1843 they got married in a Protestant church in Kreuznach.[25]

In October 1836, Marx arrived in Berlin, matriculating in the university's faculty of law and renting a room in the Mittelstrasse.[26] During the first term, Marx attended lectures of Eduard Gans who represented the progressive Hegelian standpoint, elaborated on rational development in history by emphasizing particularly its libertarian aspects, and the importance of social question, and lectures of Karl von Savigny who represented the Historical School of Law. Although studying law, he was fascinated by philosophy and looked for a way to combine the two, believing that "without philosophy nothing could be accomplished".[27] Marx became interested in the recently deceased German philosopher G. W. F. Hegel, whose ideas were then widely debated among European philosophical circles.[28] During a convalescence in Stralau, he joined the Doctor's Club (*Doktorklub*), a student group which discussed Hegelian ideas and through them became involved with a group of radical thinkers known as the Young Hegelians in 1837. They gathered around Ludwig Feuerbach and Bruno Bauer, with Marx developing a particularly close friendship with Adolf Rutenberg. Like Marx, the Young Hegelians were critical of Hegel's metaphysical assumptions, but adopted his dialectical method in order to criticise established society, politics and religion from a leftist perspective.[29] Marx's father died in May 1838, resulting in a diminished income for the family.[30] Marx had been emotionally close to his father and treasured his memory after his death.

By 1837, Marx was writing both fiction and non-fiction, having completed a short novel, *Scorpion and Felix*, a drama, *Oulanem*, as well as a number of love poems dedicated to Jenny von Westphalen, though none of this early work was published during his lifetime.[31] Marx soon abandoned fiction for other pursuits, including the study of both English and Italian, art history and the translation of Latin classics.[32] He began co-operating with Bruno Bauer on editing Hegel's *Philosophy of Religion* in 1840. Marx was also engaged in writing his doctoral thesis, *The Difference Between the Democritean and Epicurean Philosophy of Nature*,[33] which he completed in 1841. It was described as "a daring and original piece of work in which Marx set out to show

Figure 2: *Jenny von Westphalen in the 1830s*

that theology must yield to the superior wisdom of philosophy".[34] The essay was controversial, particularly among the conservative professors at the University of Berlin. Marx decided instead to submit his thesis to the more liberal University of Jena, whose faculty awarded him his PhD in April 1841.[35,36] As Marx and Bauer were both atheists, in March 1841 they began plans for a journal entitled *Archiv des Atheismus* (*Atheistic Archives*), but it never came to fruition. In July, Marx and Bauer took a trip to Bonn from Berlin. There they scandalised their class by getting drunk, laughing in church and galloping through the streets on donkeys.[37]

Marx was considering an academic career, but this path was barred by the government's growing opposition to classical liberalism and the Young Hegelians.[38] Marx moved to Cologne in 1842, where he became a journalist, writing for the radical newspaper *Rheinische Zeitung* (*Rhineland News*), expressing his early views on socialism and his developing interest in economics. Marx criticised both right-wing European governments as well as figures in the liberal and socialist movements whom he thought ineffective or counterproductive.[39] The newspaper attracted the attention of the Prussian government censors, who checked every issue for seditious material before printing, as Marx lamented: "Our newspaper has to be presented to the police to be sniffed at, and if the police nose smells anything un-Christian or un-Prussian, the newspaper is not allowed to appear".[40] After the *Rheinische Zeitung* published an article strongly criticising the Russian monarchy, Tsar Nicholas I requested it be banned and Prussia's government complied in 1843.[41]

Paris: 1843–1845

In 1843, Marx became co-editor of a new, radical leftist Parisian newspaper, the *Deutsch-Französische Jahrbücher* (*German-French Annals*), then being set up by the German socialist Arnold Ruge to bring together German and French radicals[42] and thus Marx and his wife moved to Paris in October 1843. Initially living with Ruge and his wife communally at 23 Rue Vaneau, they found the living conditions difficult, so moved out following the birth of their daughter Jenny in 1844.[43] Although intended to attract writers from both France and the German states, the *Jahrbücher* was dominated by the latter and the only non-German writer was the exiled Russian anarchist collectivist Mikhail Bakunin.[44] Marx contributed two essays to the paper, "Introduction to a Contribution to the Critique of Hegel's Philosophy of Right"[45] and "On the Jewish Question",[46] the latter introducing his belief that the proletariat were a revolutionary force and marking his embrace of communism. Only one issue was published, but it was relatively successful, largely owing to the inclusion of Heinrich Heine's satirical odes on King Ludwig of Bavaria, leading the German states to ban it and seize imported copies (Ruge nevertheless refused to fund the publication of further issues and his friendship with Marx broke down).[47] After the paper's collapse, Marx began writing for the only uncensored German-language radical newspaper left, *Vorwärts!* (*Forward!*). Based in Paris, the paper was connected to the League of the Just, a utopian socialist secret society of workers and artisans. Marx attended some of their meetings, but did not join.[48] In *Vorwärts!*, Marx refined his views on socialism based upon Hegelian and Feuerbachian ideas of dialectical materialism, at the same time criticising liberals and other socialists operating in Europe.

On 28 August 1844, Marx met the German socialist Friedrich Engels at the Café de la Régence, beginning a lifelong friendship.[49] Engels showed Marx his recently published *The Condition of the Working Class in England in 1844*,[50,51] convincing Marx that the working class would be the agent and instrument of the final revolution in history.[52] Soon, Marx and Engels were collaborating on a criticism of the philosophical ideas of Marx's former friend, Bruno Bauer. This work was published in 1845 as *The Holy Family*.[53,54] Although critical of Bauer, Marx was increasingly influenced by the ideas of the Young Hegelians Max Stirner and Ludwig Feuerbach, but eventually Marx and Engels abandoned Feuerbachian materialism as well.

Figure 3: *Friedrich Engels, whom Marx met in 1844;*
the two became lifelong friends and collaborators

During the time that he lived at 38 Rue Vanneau in Paris (from October 1843 until January 1845),[55] Marx engaged in an intensive study of political economy (Adam Smith, David Ricardo, James Mill, *etc.*),[56] the French socialists (especially Claude Henri St. Simon and Charles Fourier)[57] and the history of France.[58] The study of political economy is a study that Marx would pursue for the rest of his life[59] and would result in his major economic work—the three-volume series called *Capital*.[60] Marxism is based in large part on three influences: Hegel's dialectics, French utopian socialism and English economics. Together with his earlier study of Hegel's dialectics, the studying that Marx did during this time in Paris meant that all major components of "Marxism" were in place by the autumn of 1844.[61] Marx was constantly being pulled away from his study of political economy—not only by the usual daily demands of the time, but additionally by editing a radical newspaper and later by organising and directing the efforts of a political party during years of potentially revolutionary popular uprisings of the citizenry. Still Marx was always drawn back to his economic studies: he sought "to understand the inner workings of capitalism".[62]

An outline of "Marxism" had definitely formed in the mind of Karl Marx by late 1844. Indeed, many features of the Marxist view of the world's political economy had been worked out in great detail, but Marx needed to write down all of the details of his economic world view to further clarify the new economic theory in his own mind.[63] Accordingly, Marx wrote *The Economic and Philosophical Manuscripts*.[64] These manuscripts covered numerous topics, detailing Marx's concept of alienated labour. However, by the spring of 1845 his continued study of political economy, capital and capitalism had led Marx to the belief that the new political economic theory that he was espousing—scientific socialism—needed to be built on the base of a thoroughly developed materialistic view of the world.[65]

The *Economic and Philosophical Manuscripts of 1844* had been written between April and August 1844, but soon Marx recognised that the *Manuscripts* had been influenced by some inconsistent ideas of Ludwig Feuerbach. Accordingly, Marx recognised the need to break with Feuerbach's philosophy in favour of historical materialism, thus a year later (in April 1845) after moving from Paris to Brussels, Marx wrote his eleven "Theses on Feuerbach".[66] The "Theses on Feuerbach" are best known for Thesis 11, which states that "philosophers have only interpreted the world in various ways, the point is to change it".[67] This work contains Marx's criticism of materialism (for being contemplative), idealism (for reducing practice to theory) overall, criticising philosophy for putting abstract reality above the physical world. It thus introduced the first glimpse at Marx's historical materialism, an argument that the world is changed not by ideas but by actual, physical, material activity and practice. In 1845, after receiving a request from the Prussian king, the French government shut down *Vorwärts!*, with the interior minister, François Guizot, expelling Marx from France. At this point, Marx moved from Paris to Brussels, where Marx hoped to once again continue his study of capitalism and political economy.

Brussels: 1845–1848

Unable either to stay in France or to move to Germany, Marx decided to emigrate to Brussels in Belgium in February 1845. However, to stay in Belgium he had to pledge not to publish anything on the subject of contemporary politics. In Brussels, Marx associated with other exiled socialists from across Europe, including Moses Hess, Karl Heinzen and Joseph Weydemeyer. In April 1845, Engels moved from Barmen in Germany to Brussels to join Marx and the growing cadre of members of the League of the Just now seeking home in Brussels.[68] Later, Mary Burns, Engels' long-time companion, left Manchester, England to join Engels in Brussels.[69]

In mid-July 1845, Marx and Engels left Brussels for England to visit the leaders of the Chartists, a socialist movement in Britain. This was Marx's first trip to England and Engels was an ideal guide for the trip. Engels had already spent two years living in Manchester from November 1842[70] to August 1844.[71] Not

Figure 4: *The first edition of The Manifesto of the Communist Party, published in German in 1848*

only did Engels already know the English language,[72] he had also developed a close relationship with many Chartist leaders. Indeed, Engels was serving as a reporter for many Chartist and socialist English newspapers. Marx used the trip as an opportunity to examine the economic resources available for study in various libraries in London and Manchester.[73]

In collaboration with Engels, Marx also set about writing a book which is often seen as his best treatment of the concept of historical materialism, *The German Ideology*.[74] In this work, Marx broke with Ludwig Feuerbach, Bruno Bauer, Max Stirner and the rest of the Young Hegelians, while he also broke with Karl Grun and other "true socialists" whose philosophies were still based in part on "idealism". In *German Ideology*, Marx and Engels finally completed their philosophy, which was based solely on materialism as the sole motor force in history.[75] *German Ideology* is written in a humorously satirical form, but even this satirical form did not save the work from censorship. Like so many other early writings of his, *German Ideology* would not be published in Marx's lifetime and would be published only in 1932.[76]

After completing *German Ideology*, Marx turned to a work that was intended to clarify his own position regarding "the theory and tactics" of a truly "revolutionary proletarian movement" operating from the standpoint of a truly "scientific materialist" philosophy.[77] This work was intended to draw a distinction

Figure 5: *Marx, Engels and Marx's daughters*

between the utopian socialists and Marx's own scientific socialist philosophy. Whereas the utopians believed that people must be persuaded one person at a time to join the socialist movement, the way a person must be persuaded to adopt any different belief, Marx knew that people would tend on most occasions to act in accordance with their own economic interests, thus appealing to an entire class (the working class in this case) with a broad appeal to the class's best material interest would be the best way to mobilise the broad mass of that class to make a revolution and change society. This was the intent of the new book that Marx was planning, but to get the manuscript past the government censors he called the book *The Poverty of Philosophy* (1847)[78] and offered it as a response to the "petty bourgeois philosophy" of the French anarchist socialist Pierre-Joseph Proudhon as expressed in his book *The Philosophy of Poverty* (1840).[79]

These books laid the foundation for Marx and Engels's most famous work, a political pamphlet that has since come to be commonly known as *The Communist Manifesto*. While residing in Brussels in 1846, Marx continued his association with the secret radical organisation League of the Just.[80] As noted above, Marx thought the League to be just the sort of radical organisation that was needed to spur the working class of Europe toward the mass movement that would bring about a working class revolution.[81] However, to organise the working class into a mass movement the League had to cease its "secret" or "underground" orientation and operate in the open as a political party.[82] Members of the League eventually became persuaded in this regard. Accordingly, in June 1847 the League was reorganised by its membership into a new open "above ground" political society that appealed directly to the working classes.[83] This new open political society was called the Communist League.[84] Both Marx and Engels participated in drawing up the programme and organisational principles of the new Communist League.[85]

In late 1847, Marx and Engels began writing what was to become their most famous work — a programme of action for the Communist League. Written jointly by Marx and Engels from December 1847 to January 1848, *The Communist Manifesto* was first published on 21 February 1848.[86] *The Communist Manifesto* laid out the beliefs of the new Communist League. No longer a secret society, the Communist League wanted to make aims and intentions clear to the general public rather than hiding its beliefs as the League of the Just had been doing.[87] The opening lines of the pamphlet set forth the principal basis of Marxism: "The history of all hitherto existing society is the history of class struggles". It goes on to examine the antagonisms that Marx claimed were arising in the clashes of interest between the bourgeoisie (the wealthy capitalist class) and the proletariat (the industrial working class). Proceeding on from this, the *Manifesto* presents the argument for why the Communist League, as opposed to other socialist and liberal political parties and groups at the time, was truly acting in the interests of the proletariat to overthrow capitalist society and to replace it with socialism.[88]

Later that year, Europe experienced a series of protests, rebellions and often violent upheavals that became known as the Revolutions of 1848. In France, a revolution led to the overthrow of the monarchy and the establishment of the French Second Republic. Marx was supportive of such activity and having recently received a substantial inheritance from his father (withheld by his uncle Lionel Philips since his father's death in 1838) of either 6,000 or 5,000 francs[89] he allegedly used a third of it to arm Belgian workers who were planning revolutionary action. Although the veracity of these allegations is disputed,[90] the Belgian Ministry of Justice accused Marx of it, subsequently arresting him and he was forced to flee back to France, where with a new republican government in power he believed that he would be safe.

Cologne: 1848–1849

Temporarily settling down in Paris, Marx transferred the Communist League executive headquarters to the city and also set up a German Workers' Club with various German socialists living there.[91] Hoping to see the revolution spread to Germany, in 1848 Marx moved back to Cologne where he began issuing a handbill entitled the *Demands of the Communist Party in Germany*,[92] in which he argued for only four of the ten points of the *Communist Manifesto*, believing that in Germany at that time the bourgeoisie must overthrow the feudal monarchy and aristocracy before the proletariat could overthrow the bourgeoisie.[93] On 1 June, Marx started publication of a daily newspaper, the *Neue Rheinische Zeitung*, which he helped to finance through his recent inheritance from his father. Designed to put forward news from across Europe with his own Marxist interpretation of events, the newspaper featured Marx as a primary writer and the dominant editorial influence. Despite contributions by fellow members of the Communist League, according to Friedrich Engels it remained "a simple dictatorship by Marx".[94,95]

Whilst editor of the paper, Marx and the other revolutionary socialists were regularly harassed by the police and Marx was brought to trial on several occasions, facing various allegations including insulting the Chief Public Prosecutor, committing a press misdemeanor and inciting armed rebellion through tax boycotting, although each time he was acquitted. Meanwhile, the democratic parliament in Prussia collapsed and the king, Frederick William IV, introduced a new cabinet of his reactionary supporters, who implemented counter-revolutionary measures to expunge leftist and other revolutionary elements from the country. Consequently, the *Neue Rheinische Zeitung* was soon suppressed and Marx was ordered to leave the country on 16 May.[96] Marx returned to Paris, which was then under the grip of both a reactionary counter-revolution and a cholera epidemic and was soon expelled by the city authorities, who considered him a political threat. With his wife Jenny expecting their fourth child and not able to move back to Germany or Belgium, in August 1849 he sought refuge in London.[97]

Move to London and further writing: 1850–1860

Marx moved to London in early June 1849 and would remain based in the city for the rest of his life. The headquarters of the Communist League also moved to London. However, in the winter of 1849–1850 a split within the ranks of the Communist League occurred when a faction within it led by August Willich and Karl Schapper began agitating for an immediate uprising. Willich and Schapper believed that once the Communist League had initiated the uprising, the entire working class from across Europe would rise "spontaneously" to join it, thus creating revolution across Europe. Marx and Engels protested that such an unplanned uprising on the part of the Communist League was "adventuristic" and would be suicide for the Communist League.[98] Such an uprising as that recommended by the Schapper/Willich group would easily be crushed by the police and the armed forces of the reactionary governments of Europe. Marx maintained that this would spell doom for the Communist League itself, arguing that changes in society are not achieved overnight through the efforts and will power of a handful of men. They are instead brought about through a scientific analysis of economic conditions of society and by moving toward revolution through different stages of social development. In the present stage of development (*circa* 1850), following the defeat of the uprisings across Europe in 1848 he felt that the Communist League should encourage the working class to unite with progressive elements of the rising bourgeoisie to defeat the feudal aristocracy on issues involving demands for governmental reforms, such as a constitutional republic with freely elected assemblies and universal (male) suffrage. In other words, the working class must join with bourgeois and democratic forces to bring about the successful conclusion of the bourgeois revolution before stressing the working class agenda and a working class revolution.

After a long struggle which threatened to ruin the Communist League, Marx's opinion prevailed and eventually the Willich/Schapper group left the Communist League. Meanwhile, Marx also became heavily involved with the socialist German Workers' Educational Society.[99] The Society held their meetings in Great Windmill Street, Soho, central London's entertainment district.[100] This organisation was also racked by an internal struggle between its members, some of whom followed Marx while others followed the Schapper/Willich faction. The issues in this internal split were the same issues raised in the internal split within the Communist League, but Marx lost the fight with the Schapper/Willich faction within the German Workers' Educational Society and on 17 September 1850 resigned from the Society.[101]

New-York Daily Tribune and journalism

In the early period in London, Marx committed himself almost exclusively to revolutionary activities, such that his family endured extreme poverty. His main source of income was Engels, whose own source was his wealthy industrialist father. In Prussia as editor of his own newspaper, and contributor to others ideologically aligned, Marx could reach his audience, the working classes. In London, without finances to run a newspaper themselves, he and Engels turned to international journalism. At one stage they were being published by six newspapers from England, the United States, Prussia, Austria and South Africa.[102] Marx's principal earnings came from his work as European correspondent, from 1852 to 1862, for the *New-York Daily Tribune*,[17] and from also producing articles for more "bourgeois" newspapers. Marx had his articles translated from German by Wilhelm Pieper, until his proficiency in English had become adequate.

The *New-York Daily Tribune* had been founded in April 1841 by Horace Greeley.[103] Its editorial board contained progressive bourgeois journalists and publishers, among them George Ripley and the journalist Charles Dana, who was editor-in-chief. Dana, a fourierist and an abolitionist, was Marx's contact.

The *Tribune* was a vehicle for Marx to reach a transatlantic public. The journal had wide working-class appeal from its foundation; at two cents, it was inexpensive;[104] and, with about 50,000 copies per issue, its circulation was the widest in the United States.:[14] Its editorial ethos was progressive and its anti-slavery stance reflected Greeley's.:[82] Marx's first article for the paper, on the British parliamentary elections, was published on 21 August 1852.[105]

On 21 March 1857 Dana informed Marx that, due to the economic recession, only one article a week would be paid for, published or not; the others would be paid for only if published. Marx had sent his articles on Tuesdays and Fridays, but, that October, the *Tribune* discharged all its correspondents in Europe except Marx and B. Taylor, and reduced Marx to a weekly article. Between September and November 1860, only five were published. After a six-month interval, Marx resumed contributions in September 1861 until March 1862, when Dana wrote to inform him that there was no longer space in the *Tribune* for reports from London, due to American domestic affairs.[106] In 1868, Dana set up a rival newspaper, the *New York Sun*, at which he was editor-in-chief.[107]

In April 1857, Dana invited Marx to contribute articles, mainly on military history, to the *New American Cyclopedia*, an idea of George Ripley, Dana's friend and literary editor of the *Tribune*. In all, 67 Marx-Engels articles were published, of which 51 written by Engels, although Marx did some research for them in the British Museum.

By the late 1850s, American popular interest in European affairs waned and Marx's articles turned to topics such as the "slavery crisis" and the outbreak of the American Civil War in 1861, in the "War Between the States".[108] Between December 1851 and March 1852, Marx worked on his theoretical work about the French Revolution of 1848, titled *The Eighteenth Brumaire of Louis Napoleon*.[109] In this he explored concepts in historical materialism, class struggle, dictatorship of the proletariat, and victory of the proletariat over the bourgeois state.

The 1850s and 1860s may be said to mark a philosophical boundary distinguishing the young Marx's Hegelian idealism and the more mature Marx's scientific ideology associated with structural Marxism; however, not all scholars accept this distinction. For Marx and Engels, their experience of the Revolutions of 1848 to 1849 were formative in the development of their theory of economics and historical progression. After the "failures" of 1848, the revolutionary impetus appeared spent and not to be renewed without an economic recession. Contention arose between Marx and his fellow communists, whom he denounced as "adventurists". Marx deemed it fanciful to propose that "will power" could be sufficient to create the revolutionary conditions when in reality the economic component was the necessary requisite.

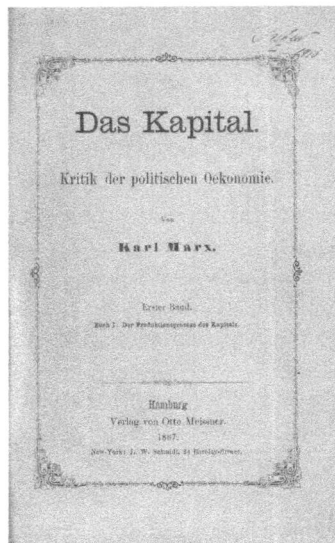

Figure 6: *The first volume of Das Kapital*

Recession in the United States' economy in 1852 gave Marx and Engels grounds for optimism for revolutionary activity. Yet, this economy was seen as too immature for a capitalist revolution. Open territories on America's western frontier dissipated the forces of social unrest. Moreover, any economic crisis arising in the United States would not lead to revolutionary contagion of the older economies of individual European nations, which were closed systems bounded by their national borders. When the so-called "Panic of 1857" in the United States spread globally, it broke all economic theory models,[110] and was the first truly global economic crisis.

Financial necessity had forced Marx to abandon economic studies in 1844 and give thirteen years to working on other projects. He had always sought to return to economics.

The First International and *Capital*

Marx continued to write articles for the *New York Daily Tribune* as long as he was sure that the *Tribune's* editorial policy was still progressive. However, the departure of Charles Dana from the paper in late 1861 and the resultant change in the editorial board brought about a new editorial policy.[111] No longer was the *Tribune* to be a strong abolitionist paper dedicated to a complete Union victory. The new editorial board supported an immediate peace between the

Union and the Confederacy in the Civil War in the United States with slavery left intact in the Confederacy. Marx strongly disagreed with this new political position and in 1863 was forced to withdraw as a writer for the *Tribune*.[112]

In 1864, Marx became involved in the International Workingmen's Association (also known as the First International), to whose General Council he was elected at its inception in 1864. In that organisation, Marx was involved in the struggle against the anarchist wing centred on Mikhail Bakunin (1814–1876). Although Marx won this contest, the transfer of the seat of the General Council from London to New York in 1872, which Marx supported, led to the decline of the International. The most important political event during the existence of the International was the Paris Commune of 1871, when the citizens of Paris rebelled against their government and held the city for two months. In response to the bloody suppression of this rebellion, Marx wrote one of his most famous pamphlets, "The Civil War in France", a defence of the Commune.[113]

Given the repeated failures and frustrations of workers' revolutions and movements, Marx also sought to understand capitalism and spent a great deal of time in the reading room of the British Museum studying and reflecting on the works of political economists and on economic data. By 1857, Marx had accumulated over 800 pages of notes and short essays on capital, landed property, wage labour, the state and foreign trade and the world market, though this work did not appear in print until 1939 under the title *Outlines of the Critique of Political Economy*.[114,115]

Finally in 1859, Marx published *A Contribution to the Critique of Political Economy*,[116] his first serious economic work. This work was intended merely as a preview of his three-volume *Das Kapital* (English title: *Capital: Critique of Political Economy*), which he intended to publish at a later date. In *A Contribution to the Critique of Political Economy*, Marx expands on the labour theory of value advocated by David Ricardo. The work was enthusiastically received, and the edition sold out quickly.[117]

The successful sales of *A Contribution to the Critique of Political Economy* stimulated Marx in the early 1860s to finish work on the three large volumes that would compose his major life's work—*Das Kapital* and the *Theories of Surplus Value*, which discussed the theoreticians of political economy, particularly Adam Smith and David Ricardo. *Theories of Surplus Value* is often referred to as the fourth volume of *Das Kapital* and constitutes one of the first comprehensive treatises on the history of economic thought. In 1867, the first volume of *Das Kapital* was published, a work which analysed the capitalist process of production. Here Marx elaborated his labour theory of value, which had been influenced by Thomas Hodgskin. Marx acknowledged Hodgskin's "admirable work" *Labour Defended against the Claims of Capital* at more than one point in *Capital*.[118] Indeed, Marx quoted Hodgskin as

Figure 7: *Marx in the 1870s*

recognising the alienation of labour that occurred under modern capitalist production. No longer was there any "natural reward of individual labour. Each
labourer produces only some part of a whole, and each part having no value
or utility of itself, there is nothing on which the labourer can seize, and say:
'This is my product, this will I keep to myself'".[119] In this first volume of *Capital*, Marx outlined his conception of surplus value and exploitation, which he
argued would ultimately lead to a falling rate of profit and the collapse of industrial capitalism. Demand for a Russian language edition of *Capital* soon
led to the printing of 3,000 copies of the book in the Russian language, which
was published on 27 March 1872. By the autumn of 1871, the entire first edition of the German language edition of *Capital* had been sold out and a second
edition was published.

Volumes II and III of *Capital* remained mere manuscripts upon which Marx
continued to work for the rest of his life. Both volumes were published by
Engels after Marx's death. Volume II of *Capital* was prepared and published
by Engels in July 1893 under the name *Capital II: The Process of Circulation
of Capital*.[120] Volume III of *Capital* was published a year later in October
1894 under the name *Capital III: The Process of Capitalist Production as
a Whole*.[121] *Theories of Surplus Value* derived from the sprawling *Economic
Manuscripts of 1861-1863*, a *second* draft for *Capital*, the latter spanning volumes 30-34 of the *Collected Works of Marx and Engels*. Specifically, *Theo-*

Figure 8: *Marx in 1882*

ries of Surplus Value runs from the latter part of the *Collected Works'* thirtieth volume through the end of their thirty-second volume;[122,123,124] meanwhile, the larger *Economic Manuscripts of 1861-1863* run from the start of the *Collected Works'* thirtieth volume through the first half of their thirty-fourth volume. The latter half of the Collected Works' thirty-fourth volume consists of the surviving fragments of the *Economic Manuscripts of 1863-1864*, which represented a *third* draft for Capital, and a large portion of which is included as an appendix to the Penguin edition of *Capital*, volume I. A German language abridged edition of *Theories of Surplus Value* was published in 1905 and in 1910. This abridged edition was translated into English and published in 1951 in London, but the complete unabridged edition of *Theories of Surplus Value* was published as the "fourth volume" of *Capital* in 1963 and 1971 in Moscow.[125]

During the last decade of his life, Marx's health declined and he became incapable of the sustained effort that had characterised his previous work. He did manage to comment substantially on contemporary politics, particularly in Germany and Russia. His *Critique of the Gotha Programme* opposed the tendency of his followers Wilhelm Liebknecht and August Bebel to compromise with the state socialism of Ferdinand Lassalle in the interests of a united socialist party. This work is also notable for another famous Marx quote: "From each according to his ability, to each according to his need".

In a letter to Vera Zasulich dated 8 March 1881, Marx contemplated the possibility of Russia's bypassing the capitalist stage of development and building communism on the basis of the common ownership of land characteristic of the village *mir*.[126] While admitting that Russia's rural "commune is the fulcrum of social regeneration in Russia", Marx also warned that in order for the mir to operate as a means for moving straight to the socialist stage without a preceding capitalist stage it "would first be necessary to eliminate the deleterious influences which are assailing it (the rural commune) from all sides". Given the elimination of these pernicious influences, Marx allowed that "normal conditions of spontaneous development" of the rural commune could exist. However, in the same letter to Vera Zasulich he points out that "at the core of the capitalist system ... lies the complete separation of the producer from the means of production". In one of the drafts of this letter, Marx reveals his growing passion for anthropology, motivated by his belief that future communism would be a return on a higher level to the communism of our prehistoric past. He wrote that "the historical trend of our age is the fatal crisis which capitalist production has undergone in the European and American countries where it has reached its highest peak, a crisis that will end in its destruction, in the return of modern society to a higher form of the most archaic type—collective production and appropriation". He added that "the vitality of primitive communities was incomparably greater than that of Semitic, Greek, Roman, *etc.* societies, and, a fortiori, that of modern capitalist societies".[127] Before he died, Marx asked Engels to write up these ideas, which were published in 1884 under the title *The Origin of the Family, Private Property and the State*.

Personal life

Family

Marx and von Westphalen had seven children together, but partly owing to the poor conditions in which they lived whilst in London, only three survived to adulthood.[128] The children were: Jenny Caroline (m. Longuet; 1844–1883); Jenny Laura (m. Lafargue; 1845–1911); Edgar (1847–1855); Henry Edward Guy ("Guido"; 1849–1850); Jenny Eveline Frances ("Franziska"; 1851–1852); Jenny Julia Eleanor (1855–1898) and one more who died before being named (July 1857). There are allegations that Marx also fathered a son, Freddy, out of wedlock by his housekeeper, Helene Demuth.

Marx frequently used pseudonyms, often when renting a house or flat, apparently to make it harder for the authorities to track him down. While in Paris, he used that of "Monsieur Ramboz", whilst in London he signed off his letters as "A. Williams". His friends referred to him as "Moor", owing to his dark

Figure 9: *Jenny Carolina and Jenny Laura Marx (1869): all the Marx daughters were named Jenny in honour of their mother, Jenny von Westphalen.*

complexion and black curly hair, while he encouraged his children to call him "Old Nick" and "Charley". He also bestowed nicknames and pseudonyms on his friends and family as well, referring to Friedrich Engels as "General", his housekeeper Helene as "Lenchen" or "Nym", while one of his daughters, Jennychen, was referred to as "Qui Qui, Emperor of China" and another, Laura, was known as "Kakadou" or "the Hottentot".

Health

Marx was afflicted by poor health (what he himself described as "the wretchedness of existence")[129] and various authors have sought to describe and explain it. His biographer Werner Blumenberg attributed it to liver and gall problems which Marx had in 1849 and from which he was never afterwards free, exacerbated by an unsuitable lifestyle. The attacks often came with headaches, eye inflammation, neuralgia in the head and rheumatic pains. A serious nervous disorder appeared in 1877 and protracted insomnia was a consequence, which Marx fought with narcotics. The illness was aggravated by excessive nocturnal work and faulty diet. Marx was fond of highly seasoned dishes, smoked fish, caviare, pickled cucumbers, "none of which are good for liver patients", but he also liked wine and liqueurs and smoked an enormous amount "and since he had no money, it was usually bad-quality cigars". From 1863, Marx complained a lot about boils: "These are very frequent with liver patients and may be due to the same causes".[130] The abscesses were so bad that Marx could neither sit nor work upright. According to Blumenberg, Marx's irritability is often found in liver patients:

The illness emphasised certain traits in his character. He argued cuttingly, his biting satire did not shrink at insults, and his expressions could be rude and cruel. Though in general Marx had a blind faith in his closest friends, nevertheless he himself complained that he was sometimes too mistrustful and unjust even to them. His verdicts, not only about enemies but even about friends, were sometimes so harsh that even less sensitive people would take offence... There must have been few whom he did not criticize like this... not even Engels was an exception.[131]

According to Princeton historian J.E. Seigel, in his late teens Marx may have had pneumonia or pleurisy, the effects of which led to his being exempted from Prussian military service. In later life whilst working on *Capital* (which he never completed),[132] Marx suffered from a trio of afflictions. A liver ailment, probably hereditary, was aggravated by overwork, bad diet and lack of sleep. Inflammation of the eyes was induced by too much work at night. A third affliction, eruption of carbuncles or boils, "was probably brought on by general physical debility to which the various features of Marx's style of life — alcohol, tobacco, poor diet, and failure to sleep — all contributed. Engels often exhorted Marx to alter this dangerous regime". In Professor Seigel's thesis, what lay behind this punishing sacrifice of his health may have been guilt about self-involvement and egoism, originally induced in Karl Marx by his father.[133]

In 2007, a retrodiagnosis of Marx's skin disease was made by dermatologist Sam Shuster of Newcastle University and for Shuster the most probable explanation was that Marx suffered not from liver problems, but from hidradenitis suppurativa, a recurring infective condition arising from blockage of apocrine ducts opening into hair follicles. This condition, which was not described in the English medical literature until 1933 (hence would not have been known to Marx's physicians), can produce joint pain (which could be misdiagnosed as rheumatic disorder) and painful eye conditions. To arrive at his retrodiagnosis, Shuster considered the primary material: the Marx correspondence published in the 50 volumes of the *Marx/Engels Collected Works*. There, "although the skin lesions were called 'furuncules', 'boils' and 'carbuncles' by Marx, his wife and his physicians, they were too persistent, recurrent, destructive and site-specific for that diagnosis". The sites of the persistent 'carbuncles'

Figure 10: *Tomb of Karl Marx, East Highgate Cemetery, London*

were noted repeatedly in the armpits, groins, perianal, genital (penis and scrotum) and suprapubic regions and inner thighs, "favoured sites of hidradenitis suppurativa" Professor Shuster claimed the diagnosis "can now be made definitively".[134]

Shuster went on to consider the potential psychosocial effects of the disease, noting that the skin is an organ of communication and that hidradenitis suppurativa produces much psychological distress, including loathing and disgust and depression of self-image, mood and well-being, feelings for which Shuster found "much evidence" in the Marx correspondence. Professor Shuster went on to ask himself whether the mental effects of the disease affected Marx's work and even helped him to develop his theory of alienation.[135]

Death

Following the death of his wife Jenny in December 1881, Marx developed a catarrh that kept him in ill health for the last 15 months of his life. It eventually brought on the bronchitis and pleurisy that killed him in London on 14 March 1883 (age 64), dying a stateless person. Family and friends in London buried his body in Highgate Cemetery (East), London, on 17 March 1883 in an area reserved for agnostics and atheists (George Eliot's grave is nearby). There were between nine and eleven mourners at his funeral.[136]

Several of his closest friends spoke at his funeral, including Wilhelm Liebknecht and Friedrich Engels. Engels' speech included the passage: <templatestyles src="Template:Quote/styles.css"/>

> On the 14th of March, at a quarter to three in the afternoon, the greatest living thinker ceased to think. He had been left alone for scarcely two minutes, and when we came back we found him in his armchair, peacefully gone to sleep—but forever.

Marx's surviving daughters Eleanor and Laura, as well as Charles Longuet and Paul Lafargue, Marx's two French socialist sons-in-law, were also in attendance. He had been predeceased by his wife and his eldest daughter, the latter dying a few months earlier in January 1883. Liebknecht, a founder and leader of the German Social Democratic Party, gave a speech in German and Longuet, a prominent figure in the French working-class movement, made a short statement in French. Two telegrams from workers' parties in France and Spain were also read out. Together with Engels's speech, this constituted the entire programme of the funeral. Non-relatives attending the funeral included three communist associates of Marx: Friedrich Lessner, imprisoned for three years after the Cologne communist trial of 1852; G. Lochner, whom Engels described as "an old member of the Communist League"; and Carl Schorlemmer, a professor of chemistry in Manchester, a member of the Royal Society and a communist activist involved in the 1848 Baden revolution. Another attendee of the funeral was Ray Lankester, a British zoologist who would later become a prominent academic.

Upon his own death in 1895, Engels left Marx's two surviving daughters a "significant portion" of his considerable estate (valued in 2011 at US$4.8m).

Marx and his family were reburied on a new site nearby in November 1954. The tomb at the new site, unveiled on 14 March 1956, bears the carved message: "Workers of All Lands Unite", the final line of The Communist Manifesto; and, from the 11th "Thesis on Feuerbach" (as edited by Engels), "The philosophers have only interpreted the world in various ways—the point however is to change it". The Communist Party of Great Britain had the monument with a portrait bust by Laurence Bradshaw erected and Marx's original tomb had only humble adornment. In 1970, there was an unsuccessful attempt to destroy the monument using a homemade bomb.[137]

The Marxist historian Eric Hobsbawm remarked: "One cannot say Marx died a failure" because although he had not achieved a large following of disciples in Britain, his writings had already begun to make an impact on the leftist movements in Germany and Russia. Within 25 years of his death, the continental European socialist parties that acknowledged Marx's influence on their politics were each gaining between 15 and 47 per cent in those countries with representative democratic elections.[138]

Thought

Part of a series on

Marxism

- 🏴 Socialism portal
- ⚒ Communism portal
- 🎓 Philosophy portal

- v
- t
- e[139]

Influences

Marx's thought demonstrates influences from many thinkers including, but not limited to:

- Lycurgus' philosophy, including the forceful and equal redistribution of resources (land) and the equality of all citizens[140]
- Georg Wilhelm Friedrich Hegel's philosophy
- The classical political economy (economics) of Adam Smith and David Ricardo
- French socialist thought, in particular the thought of Jean-Jacques Rousseau, Henri de Saint-Simon, Pierre-Joseph Proudhon and Charles Fourier
- Earlier German philosophical materialism among the Young Hegelians, particularly that of Ludwig Feuerbach and Bruno Bauer, as well as the French materialism of the late 18th century, including Diderot, Claude Adrien Helvétius and d'Holbach

- The working class analysis by Friedrich Engels, as well as the early descriptions of class provided by French liberals and Saint-Simonians such as François Guizot and Augustin Thierry
- Marx's Judaic legacy has been identified as formative to both his moral outlook[141] and his materialist philosophy.[142]

Marx's view of history, which came to be called historical materialism (controversially adapted as the philosophy of dialectical materialism by Engels and Lenin), certainly shows the influence of Hegel's claim that one should view reality (and history) dialectically. However, Hegel had thought in idealist terms, putting ideas in the forefront, whereas Marx sought to rewrite dialectics in materialist terms, arguing for the primacy of matter over idea. Where Hegel saw the "spirit" as driving history, Marx saw this as an unnecessary mystification, obscuring the reality of humanity and its physical actions shaping the world. He wrote that Hegelianism stood the movement of reality on its head, and that one needed to set it upon its feet. Despite his dislike of mystical terms, Marx used Gothic language in several of his works: in *The Communist Manifesto* he proclaims "A spectre is haunting Europe—the spectre of communism. All the powers of old Europe have entered into a holy alliance to exorcise this spectre", and in *The Capital* he refers to capital as "necromancy that surrounds the products of labour".

Though inspired by French socialist and sociological thought, Marx criticised utopian socialists, arguing that their favoured small-scale socialistic communities would be bound to marginalisation and poverty and that only a large-scale change in the economic system can bring about real change.

The other important contribution to Marx's revision of Hegelianism came from Engels's book, *The Condition of the Working Class in England in 1844*, which led Marx to conceive of the historical dialectic in terms of class conflict and to see the modern working class as the most progressive force for revolution.

Marx believed that he could study history and society scientifically and discern tendencies of history and the resulting outcome of social conflicts. Some followers of Marx therefore concluded that a communist revolution would inevitably occur. However, Marx famously asserted in the eleventh of his "Theses on Feuerbach" that "philosophers have only interpreted the world, in various ways; the point however is to change it" and he clearly dedicated himself to trying to alter the world.

Philosophy and social thought

Marx's polemic with other thinkers often occurred through critique and thus he has been called "the first great user of critical method in social sciences". He criticised speculative philosophy, equating metaphysics with ideology. By adopting this approach, Marx attempted to separate key findings from ideological biases. This set him apart from many contemporary philosophers.

Human nature

<templatestyles src="Multiple_image/styles.css" />

The philosophers G. W. F. Hegel and Ludwig Feuerbach, whose ideas on dialectics heavily influenced Marx

Like Tocqueville, who described a faceless and bureaucratic despotism with no identifiable despot,[143] Marx also broke with classical thinkers who spoke of a single tyrant and with Montesquieu, who discussed the nature of the single despot. Instead, Marx set out to analyse "the despotism of capital".[144] Fundamentally, Marx assumed that human history involves transforming human nature, which encompasses both human beings and material objects. Humans recognise that they possess both actual and potential selves.[145,146] For both Marx and Hegel, self-development begins with an experience of internal alienation stemming from this recognition, followed by a realisation that the actual self, as a subjective agent, renders its potential counterpart an object to be apprehended. Marx further argues that by moulding nature[147] in desired ways[148] the subject takes the object as its own and thus permits the individual to be actualised as fully human. For Marx, the human nature—*Gattungswesen*, or species-being—exists as a function of human labour. Fundamental to Marx's idea of meaningful labour is the proposition that in order for a subject to come

Figure 11: *A monument dedicated to Marx and Engels in Shanghai, China*

to terms with its alienated object it must first exert influence upon literal, material objects in the subject's world. Marx acknowledges that Hegel "grasps the nature of work and comprehends objective man, authentic because actual, as the result of his *own work*",[149] but characterises Hegelian self-development as unduly "spiritual" and abstract.[150] Marx thus departs from Hegel by insisting that "the fact that man is a corporeal, actual, sentient, objective being with natural capacities means that he has actual, sensuous objects for his nature as objects of his life-expression, or that he can only express his life in actual sensuous objects".[151] Consequently, Marx revises Hegelian "work" into material "labour" and in the context of human capacity to transform nature the term "labour power".

Labour, class struggle and false consciousness

<templatestyles src="Template:Quote/styles.css"/>

The history of all hitherto existing society is the history of class struggles.

—*Karl Marx, The Communist Manifesto*

Marx had a special concern with how people relate to their own labour power. He wrote extensively about this in terms of the problem of alienation. As with the dialectic, Marx began with a Hegelian notion of alienation but developed a more materialist conception. Capitalism mediates social relationships of production (such as among workers or between workers and capitalists) through commodities, including labour, that are bought and sold on the market. For Marx, the possibility that one may give up ownership of one's own labour—one's capacity to transform the world—is tantamount to being alienated from one's own nature and it is a spiritual loss. Marx described this loss as commodity fetishism, in which the things that people produce, commodities, appear to have a life and movement of their own to which humans and their behaviour merely adapt.

Commodity fetishism provides an example of what Engels called "false consciousness", which relates closely to the understanding of ideology. By "ideology", Marx and Engels meant ideas that reflect the interests of a particular class at a particular time in history, but which contemporaries see as universal and eternal. Marx and Engels's point was not only that such beliefs are at best half-truths, as they serve an important political function. Put another way, the control that one class exercises over the means of production includes not only the production of food or manufactured goods, but also the production of ideas (this provides one possible explanation for why members of a subordinate class may hold ideas contrary to their own interests). An example of this sort of analysis is Marx's understanding of religion, summed up in a passage from the preface[152] to his 1843 *Contribution to the Critique of Hegel's Philosophy of Right*: <templatestyles src="Template:Quote/styles.css"/>

> *Religious suffering is, at one and the same time, the expression of real suffering and a protest against real suffering. Religion is the sigh of the oppressed creature, the heart of a heartless world, and the soul of soulless conditions. It is the opium of the people. The abolition of religion as the illusory happiness of the people is the demand for their real happiness. To call on them to give up their illusions about their condition is to call on them to give up a condition that requires illusions.*

Whereas his Gymnasium senior thesis at the Gymnasium zu Trier argued that religion had as its primary social aim the promotion of solidarity, here Marx sees the social function of religion in terms of highlighting/preserving political and economic *status quo* and inequality.

Marx was an outspoken opponent of child labour,[153] saying that British industries "could but live by sucking blood, and children's blood too", and that U.S. capital was financed by the "capitalized blood of children".

Figure 12: *Mural by Diego Rivera showing Karl Marx. In the National Palace in Mexico City.*

Economy, history and society

Marx's thoughts on labour were related to the primacy he gave to the economic relation in determining the society's past, present and future (see also economic determinism). Accumulation of capital shapes the social system. For Marx, social change was about conflict between opposing interests, driven in the background by economic forces. This became the inspiration for the body of works known as the conflict theory. In his evolutionary model of history, he argued that human history began with free, productive and creative work that was over time coerced and dehumanised, a trend most apparent under capitalism. Marx noted that this was not an intentional process, rather no individual or even state can go against the forces of economy.

The organisation of society depends on means of production. The means of production are all things required to produce material goods, such as land, natural resources and technology but not human labor. The relations of production are the social relationships people enter into as they acquire and use the means of production. Together, these compose the mode of production and Marx distinguished historical eras in terms of modes of production. Marx differentiated between base and superstructure, where the base (or substructure) is the economic system and superstructure is the cultural and political

Figure 13: *Memorial to Karl Marx in Moscow, whose inscription reads: "Proletarians of all countries, unite!"*

system. Marx regarded this mismatch between economic base and social superstructure as a major source of social disruption and conflict.

Despite Marx's stress on critique of capitalism and discussion of the new communist society that should replace it, his explicit critique is guarded, as he saw it as an improved society compared to the past ones (slavery and feudalism). Marx never clearly discusses issues of morality and justice, but scholars agree that his work contained implicit discussion of those concepts.

Marx's view of capitalism was two-sided. On one hand, in the 19th century's deepest critique of the dehumanising aspects of this system he noted that defining features of capitalism include alienation, exploitation and recurring, cyclical depressions leading to mass unemployment. On the other hand, he characterized capitalism as "revolutionising, industrialising and universalising qualities of development, growth and progressivity" (by which Marx meant industrialisation, urbanisation, technological progress, increased productivity and growth, rationality and scientific revolution) that are responsible for progress. Marx considered the capitalist class to be one of the most revolutionary in history because it constantly improved the means of production, more so than any other class in history and was responsible for the overthrow of feudalism. Capitalism can stimulate considerable growth because the capitalist has an incentive to reinvest profits in new technologies and capital equipment.

According to Marx, capitalists take advantage of the difference between the labour market and the market for whatever commodity the capitalist can produce. Marx observed that in practically every successful industry, input unit-costs are lower than output unit-prices. Marx called the difference "surplus value" and argued that it was based on surplus labour, the difference between what it costs to keep workers alive and what they can produce. Although Marx describes capitalists as vampires sucking worker's blood, he notes that drawing profit is "by no means an injustice" and that capitalists cannot go against the system. The problem is the "cancerous cell" of capital, understood not as property or equipment, but the relations between workers and owners—the economic system in general.

At the same time, Marx stressed that capitalism was unstable and prone to periodic crises. He suggested that over time capitalists would invest more and more in new technologies and less and less in labour. Since Marx believed that profit derived from surplus value appropriated from labour, he concluded that the rate of profit would fall as the economy grows. Marx believed that increasingly severe crises would punctuate this cycle of growth and collapse. Moreover, he believed that in the long-term, this process would enrich and empower the capitalist class and impoverish the proletariat. In section one of *The Communist Manifesto*, Marx describes feudalism, capitalism and the role internal social contradictions play in the historical process: <templatestyles src="Template:Quote/styles.css"/>

> *We see then: the means of production and of exchange, on whose foundation the bourgeoisie built itself up, were generated in feudal society. At a certain stage in the development of these means of production and of exchange, the conditions under which feudal society produced and exchanged ... the feudal relations of property became no longer compatible with the already developed productive forces; they became so many fetters. They had to be burst asunder; they were burst asunder. Into their place stepped free competition, accompanied by a social and political constitution adapted in it, and the economic and political sway of the bourgeois class. A similar movement is going on before our own eyes ... The productive forces at the disposal of society no longer tend to further the development of the conditions of bourgeois property; on the contrary, they have become too powerful for these conditions, by which they are fettered, and so soon as they overcome these fetters, they bring order into the whole of bourgeois society, endanger the existence of bourgeois property.*

Marx believed that those structural contradictions within capitalism necessitate its end, giving way to socialism, or a post-capitalistic, communist society: <templatestyles src="Template:Quote/styles.css"/>

Figure 14: *Outside a factory in Oldham. Marx believed that industrial workers (the proletariat) would rise up around the world.*

The development of Modern Industry, therefore, cuts from under its feet the very foundation on which the bourgeoisie produces and appropriates products. What the bourgeoisie, therefore, produces, above all, are its own grave-diggers. Its fall and the victory of the proletariat are equally inevitable.

Thanks to various processes overseen by capitalism, such as urbanisation, the working class, the proletariat, should grow in numbers and develop class consciousness, in time realising that they can and must change the system. Marx believed that if the proletariat were to seize the means of production, they would encourage social relations that would benefit everyone equally, abolishing exploiting class and introduce a system of production less vulnerable to cyclical crises. Marx argued in *The German Ideology* that capitalism will end through the organised actions of an international working class: <templatestyles src="Template:Quote/styles.css"/>

Communism is for us not a state of affairs which is to be established, an ideal to which reality will have to adjust itself. We call communism the real movement which abolishes the present state of things. The conditions of this movement result from the premises now in existence.

In this new society, the alienation would end and humans would be free to act without being bound by the labour market. It would be a democratic society, enfranchising the entire population. In such a utopian world, there would also be little need for a state, whose goal was previously to enforce the alienation. Marx theorised that between capitalism and the establishment of a socialist/communist system, would exist a period of dictatorship of the proletariat—where the working class holds political power and forcibly socialises the means of production. As he wrote in his *Critique of the Gotha Program*, "between capitalist and communist society there lies the period of the revolutionary transformation of the one into the other. Corresponding to this is also a political transition period in which the state can be nothing but the revolutionary dictatorship of the proletariat". While he allowed for the possibility of peaceful transition in some countries with strong democratic institutional structures (such as Britain, the United States and the Netherlands), he suggested that in other countries in which workers cannot "attain their goal by peaceful means" the "lever of our revolution must be force".[154]

International relations

Marx viewed Russia as the main counter-revolutionary threat to European revolutions.[155] During the Crimean War, Marx backed the Ottoman Empire and its allies Britain and France against Russia. He was absolutely opposed to Pan-Slavism, viewing it as an instrument of Russian foreign policy. Marx had considered the Slavic nations except Poles as 'counter-revolutionary'. Marx and Engels published in the *Neue Rheinische Zeitung* in February 1849:

<templatestyles src="Template:Quote/styles.css"/>

> *To the sentimental phrases about brotherhood which we are being offered here on behalf of the most counter-revolutionary nations of Europe, we reply that hatred of Russians was and still is the primary revolutionary passion among Germans; that since the revolution [of 1848] hatred of Czechs and Croats has been added, and that only by the most determined use of terror against these Slav peoples can we, jointly with the Poles and Magyars, safeguard the revolution. We know where the enemies of the revolution are concentrated, viz. in Russia and the Slav regions of Austria, and no fine phrases, no allusions to an undefined democratic future for these countries can deter us from treating our enemies as enemies. Then there will be a struggle, an "inexorable life-and-death struggle", against those Slavs who betray the revolution; an annihilating fight and ruthless terror — not in the interests of Germany, but in the interests of the revolution!*"[156]

Marx and Engels sympathised with the Narodnik revolutionaries of the 1860s and 1870s. When the Russian revolutionaries assassinated Tsar Alexander II

Figure 15: *CPI(M) mural in Kerala, India*

of Russia, Marx expressed the hope that the assassination foreshadowed 'the formation of a Russian commune'.[157] Marx supported the Polish uprisings against tsarist Russia. He said in a speech in London in 1867:

<templatestyles src="Template:Quote/styles.css"/>

> *In the first place the policy of Russia is changeless... Its methods, its tactics, its manoeuvres may change, but the polar star of its policy – world domination – is a fixed star. In our times only a civilised government ruling over barbarian masses can hatch out such a plan and execute it. ... There is but one alternative for Europe. Either Asiatic barbarism, under Muscovite direction, will burst around its head like an avalanche, or else it must re-establish Poland, thus putting twenty million heroes between itself and Asia and gaining a breathing spell for the accomplishment of its social regeneration.[158]*

Marx supported the cause of Irish independence. In 1867, he wrote Engels: "I used to think the separation of Ireland from England impossible. I now think it inevitable. The English working class will never accomplish anything until it has got rid of Ireland. ... English reaction in England had its roots ... in the subjugation of Ireland."[159]

Marx spent some time in French Algeria, which had been invaded and made a French colony in 1830, and had opportunity to observe life in colonial North

Africa. He wrote about the colonial justice system, in which "a form of torture has been used (and this happens 'regularly') to extract confessions from the Arabs; naturally it is done (like the English in India) by the 'police'; the judge is supposed to know nothing at all about it." Marx was surprised by the arrogance of many European settlers in Algiers and wrote in a letter: "when a European colonist dwells among the 'lesser breeds,' either as a settler or even on business, he generally regards himself as even more inviolable than handsome William I [a Prussian king]. Still, when it comes to bare-faced arrogance and presumptuousness vis-à-vis the 'lesser breeds,' the British and Dutch outdo the French."

According to the *Stanford Encyclopedia of Philosophy*: "Marx's analysis of colonialism as a progressive force bringing modernization to a backward feudal society sounds like a transparent rationalization for foreign domination. His account of British domination, however, reflects the same ambivalence that he shows towards capitalism in Europe. In both cases, Marx recognizes the immense suffering brought about during the transition from feudal to bourgeois society while insisting that the transition is both necessary and ultimately progressive. He argues that the penetration of foreign commerce will cause a social revolution in India."

Marx discussed British colonial rule in India in the *New York Herald Tribune* in June 1853:

<templatestyles src="Template:Quote/styles.css"/>

> *There cannot remain any doubt but that the misery inflicted by the British on Hindostan [India] is of an essentially different and infinitely more intensive kind than all Hindostan had to suffer before. England has broken down the entire framework of Indian society, without any symptoms of reconstitution yet appearing... [however], we must not forget that these idyllic village communities, inoffensive though they may appear, had always been the solid foundation of Oriental despotism, that they restrained the human mind within the smallest possible compass, making it the unresisting tool of superstition.*

Legacy

Marx's ideas have had a profound impact on world politics and intellectual thought.[160] Followers of Marx have often debated amongst themselves over how to interpret Marx's writings and apply his concepts to the modern world. The legacy of Marx's thought has become contested between numerous tendencies, each of which sees itself as Marx's most accurate interpreter. In the political realm, these tendencies include Leninism, Marxism–Leninism, Trotskyism, Maoism, Luxemburgism and libertarian Marxism. Various currents

Figure 16: *Karl Marx and Friedrich Engels monument in Marx-Engels-Forum, Berlin-Mitte, Germany*

have also developed in academic Marxism, often under influence of other views, resulting in structuralist Marxism, historical Marxism, phenomenological Marxism, analytical Marxism and Hegelian Marxism.

From an academic perspective, Marx's work contributed to the birth of modern sociology. He has been cited as one of the 19th century's three masters of the "school of suspicion" alongside Friedrich Nietzsche and Sigmund Freud[161] and as one of the three principal architects of modern social science along with Émile Durkheim and Max Weber. In contrast to other philosophers, Marx offered theories that could often be tested with the scientific method. Both Marx and Auguste Comte set out to develop scientifically justified ideologies in the wake of European secularisation and new developments in the philosophies of history and science. Working in the Hegelian tradition, Marx rejected Comtean sociological positivism in attempt to develop a *science of society*. Karl Löwith considered Marx and Søren Kierkegaard to be the two greatest Hegelian philosophical successors.[162] In modern sociological theory, Marxist sociology is recognised as one of the main classical perspectives. Isaiah Berlin considers Marx the true founder of modern sociology "in so far as anyone can claim the title".[163] Beyond social science, he has also had a lasting legacy in philosophy, literature, the arts and the humanities.[164,165]

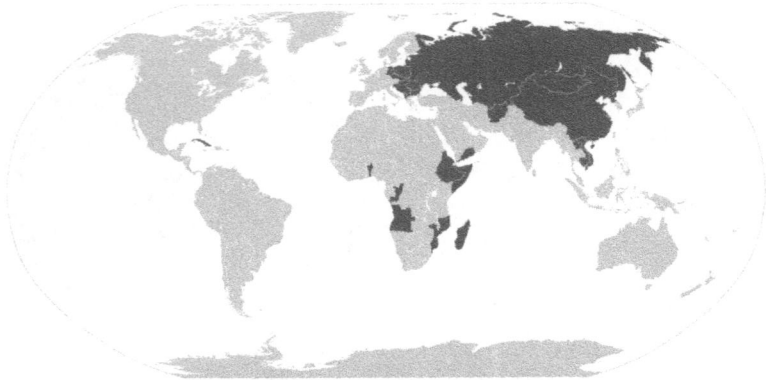

Figure 17: *Map of countries that declared themselves to be socialist states under the Marxist–Leninist or Maoist definition between 1979 and 1983, which marked the greatest territorial extent of socialist states*

Social theorists of the 20th and 21st centuries have pursued two main strategies in response to Marx. One move has been to reduce it to its analytical core, known as analytical Marxism. Another, more common, move has been to dilute the explanatory claims of Marx's social theory and emphasise the "relative autonomy" of aspects of social and economic life not directly related to Marx's central narrative of interaction between the development of the "forces of production" and the succession of "modes of production". Such has been for example the neo-Marxist theorising adopted by historians inspired by Marx's social theory, such as E. P. Thompson and Eric Hobsbawm. It has also been a line of thinking pursued by thinkers and activists like Antonio Gramsci who have sought to understand the opportunities and the difficulties of transformative political practice, seen in the light of Marxist social theory.[166,167,168,169] Marx's ideas would also have a profound influence on subsequent artists and art history, with avant-garde movements across literature, visual art, music, film and theater.[170]

Politically, Marx's legacy is more complex. Throughout the 20th century, revolutions in dozens of countries labelled themselves "Marxist"—most notably the Russian Revolution, which led to the founding of the Soviet Union. Major world leaders including Vladimir Lenin, Mao Zedong, Fidel Castro, Salvador Allende, Josip Broz Tito, Kwame Nkrumah, Jawaharlal Nehru,[171] Nelson Mandela,[172] Xi Jinping,[173] Jean-Claude Juncker and Thomas Sankara all cited Marx as an influence. Beyond where Marxist revolutions took place, Marx's ideas informed political parties worldwide. In countries associated

Figure 18: *Karl Marx statue in Trier, Germany*

Figure 19: *Karl Marx statue in Trier - label*

with some Marxist claims have led political opponents to blame Marx for millions of deaths, but the fidelity of these varied revolutionaries, leaders and parties to Marx's work is highly contested and rejected by many Marxists. It is now common to distinguish between the legacy and influence of Marx specifically and the legacy and influence of those who shaped his ideas for political purposes.

Two centuries after his birth Marx remains both controversial and relevant, as the unveiling of a 4.5m statue of him (given by China, sculpted by Wu Weishan) in his birthplace of Trier, Germany in 2018 demonstrates. In 2017 a feature film, *The Young Karl Marx*, featuring Marx, his wife Jenny Marx, and his collaborator Freidrich Engels, among other revolutionaries and intellectuals prior to the revolutions of 1848 received good reviews both for its historical accuracy and its brio in treating the intellectual life.

In May 2018, European Commission President Jean-Claude Juncker attended
the event in Karl Marx's hometown of Trier, Germany, at which a statue of
Marx, donated by the Chinese government, was unveiled. Juncker defended
Marx, saying that "Karl Marx was a philosopher, who thought into the future,
had creative aspirations, and today he stands for things, which is he not responsible for and which he didn't cause, because many of the things he wrote
down were redrafted into the opposite."[174]

Honors

- Hungary issued a postage stamp on 1 May 1953 on account of the 70th
  death anniversary of Karl Marx.[279]
- Hungary issued a commemorative postage stamp on 6 November 1964 on
  the occasion of centenary of 1st Socialist International.[280]
- India issued a stamp on 5 May 1983.[281]
- Russia issued two stamps on 5 April 2018.[282]
- On 10 October 1983 Vietnam issued two stamps.[283]
- In March 1933 Soviet Union issued three stamps.[284]

There are many other postage stamps; at least 22 countries issued postage
stamps in his honor.

Selected bibliography

- *The Philosophical Manifesto of the Historical School of Law*, 1842
- *Critique of Hegel's Philosophy of Right*, 1843
- "On the Jewish Question", 1843
- "Notes on James Mill", 1844
- *Economic and Philosophic Manuscripts of 1844*, 1844
- *The Holy Family*, 1845
- "Theses on Feuerbach", 1845
- *The German Ideology*, 1845
- *The Poverty of Philosophy*, 1847
- "Wage Labour and Capital", 1847
- *Manifesto of the Communist Party*, 1848
- *The Class Struggles in France*, 1850
- *The Eighteenth Brumaire of Louis Napoleon*, 1852
- *Grundrisse*, 1857
- *A Contribution to the Critique of Political Economy*, 1859
- *Writings on the U.S. Civil War*, 1861
- *Theories of Surplus Value*, 3 volumes, 1862
- "Value, Price and Profit", 1865

- *Capital*, Volume I (*Das Kapital*), 1867
- "The Civil War in France", 1871
- *Critique of the Gotha Program*, 1875
- "Notes on Adolph Wagner", 1883
- *Capital*, Volume II (posthumously published by Engels), 1885
- *Capital*, Volume III (posthumously published by Engels), 1894

References

279.   colnect.com/en/stamps/stamp/178779-Karl_Marx_1818-1883_philosopher-Karl_Marx-Hungary.   Catalog codes: Michel HU 1305C, Stamp Number HU 1042, Yvert et Tellier HU 1079A. 280.   colnect.com/en/stamps/stamp/176915-Karl_Marx_1818-1893_politician-Personalities-Hungary.   Catalog codes: Michel HU 2068A, Stamp Number HU 1583, Yvert et Tellier HU 1680, AFA number HU 2024.   281.   colnect.com/en/stamps/list/country/8663-India/item_name/karl+Marx.   Catalog codes: Mi:IN 950, Sn:IN 1017, Yt:IN 761, Sg:IN 1084.   282.   colnect.com/en/stamps/list/country/2650-Russia/year/2018/item_name/karl+Marx.   Catalog   codes: Col:RU   2018-18   and   Col:RU   2018-18KB   (Mini-sheet).   283.   colnect.com/en/stamps/list/country/8150-Vietnam/year/1983/item_name/karl+Marx.   Catalog   codes: Mi:VN 1367,   Sn:VN   1317,   Yt:VN   462   and   Catalog codes: Mi:VN 1368,   Yt:VN   463.   284.   colnect.com/en/stamps/list/country/2652-Soviet_Union_USSR/year/1933/item_name/karl+Marx.   Catalog codes: Mi:SU 424X-26X, Sn:SU 480-82, Yt:SU 473-75, Sg:SU 603-05, AFA:SU 431-33.

Bibliography

<templatestyles src="Template:Refbegin/styles.css" />

Calhoun, Craig J. (2002). *Classical Sociological Theory*[175]. Oxford: Wiley-Blackwell. ISBN 978-0-631-21348-2.

Hobsbawm, Eric (2011). *How to Change the World: Tales of Marx and Marxism*. London: Little, Brown. ISBN 978-1-4087-0287-1.

McLellan, David (2006). *Karl Marx: A Biography* (fourth edition). Hampshire: Palgrave MacMillan. ISBN 978-1403997302.

Nicolaievsky, Boris; Maenchen-Helfen, Otto (1976) [1936]. *Karl Marx: Man and Fighter*. trans. Gwenda David and Eric Mosbacher. Harmondsworth and New York: Pelican. ISBN 978-1-4067-2703-6.

Schwarzschild, Leopold (1986) [1948]. *The Red Prussian: Life and Legend of Karl Marx*. Pickwick Books Ltd. ISBN 978-0948859007.

Singer, Peter (1980). *Marx*. Oxford: Oxford University Press. ISBN 978-0-19-287510-5.

Sperber, Jonathan (2013). *Karl Marx: A Nineteenth-Century Life*. W. W. Norton & Co. ISBN 978-0871404671.

Stedman Jones, Gareth (2016). *Karl Marx: Greatness and Illusion*. London: Allen Lane. ISBN 978-0-713-99904-4.

Stokes, Philip (2004). *Philosophy: 100 Essential Thinkers*. Kettering: Index Books. ISBN 978-0-572-02935-7.

Vygodsky, Vitaly (1973). *The Story of a Great Discovery: How Karl Marx wrote "Capital"*[176]. Verlag Die Wirtschaft.

Wheen, Francis (2001). *Karl Marx*. London: Fourth Estate. ISBN 978-1-85702-637-5.

Further reading

<templatestyles src="Template:Refbegin/styles.css" />

Biographies

* Barnett, Vincent. *Marx* (Routledge, 2009)
* Berlin, Isaiah. *Karl Marx: His Life and Environment* (Oxford University Press, 1963) ISBN 0-19-520052-7
* Blumenberg, Werner (2000). *Karl Marx: An Illustrated Biography*. trans. Douglas Scott. London; New York: Verso. ISBN 978-1-85984-254-6.
* Gemkow, Heinrich. *Karl Marx: A Biography*[177]. Dresden: Verlag Zeit im Bild. 1968.
* Hobsbawm, E. J. (2004). "Marx, Karl Heinrich". *Oxford Dictionary of National Biography* (online ed.). Oxford University Press. doi: 10.1093/ref:odnb/39021[178]. (Subscription or UK public library membership[179] required.)
* Lenin, Vladimir (1967) [1913]. *Karl Marx: A Brief Biographical Sketch with an Exposition of Marxism*[180]. Peking: Foreign Languages Press.
* McLellan, David. *Karl Marx: his Life and Thought* Harper & Row, 1973 ISBN 978-0-06-012829-6
* Mehring, Franz. *Karl Marx: The Story of His Life* (Routledge, 2003)
* McLellan, David. *Marx before Marxism* (1980), Macmillan, ISBN 978-0-333-27882-6

- Rubel, Maximilien. *Marx Without Myth: A Chronological Study of his Life and Work* (Blackwell, 1975) ISBN 0-631-15780-8
- Segrillo, Angelo. *Karl Marx: An Overview of his Biographies*[181] (LEA Working Paper Series, n° 3, Jan. 2018).
- Sperber, Jonathan. *Karl Marx: A Nineteenth-Century Life* (W.W. Norton & Company; 2013) 648 pages; by a leading academic scholar
- Stedman Jones, Gareth. *Karl Marx: Greatness and Illusion* (Allen Lane, 2016). ISBN 978-0-713-99904-4.
- Walker, Frank Thomas. 'Karl Marx: a Bibliographic and Political Biography. *(bj.publications), 2009.*
- Wheen, Francis. *Karl Marx: A Life*[182], (Fourth Estate, 1999), ISBN 1-85702-637-3

Commentaries on Marx

- Althusser, Louis. *For Marx.* London: Verso, 2005.
- Althusser, Louis and Balibar, Étienne. *Reading Capital.* London: Verso, 2009.
- Attali, Jacques. *Karl Marx or the thought of the world.* 2005
- Avineri, Shlomo. *The Social and Political Thought of Karl Marx* (Cambridge University Press, 1968) ISBN 0-521-09619-7
- Axelos, Kostas. *Alienation, Praxis, and Techne in the Thought of Karl Marx* (translated by Ronald Bruzina, University of Texas Press, 1976).
- Blackledge, Paul. *Reflections on the Marxist Theory of History* (Manchester University Press, 2006)
- Blackledge, Paul. *Marxism and Ethics* (SUNY Press, 2012)
- Bottomore, Tom, ed. *A Dictionary of Marxist Thought.* Oxford: Blackwell, 1998.
- Callinicos, Alex (2010) [1983]. *The Revolutionary Ideas of Karl Marx.* Bloomsbury, London: Bookmarks. ISBN 978-1-905192-68-7.
- Cleaver, Harry. *Reading Capital Politically* (AK Press, 2000)
- G. A. Cohen. *Karl Marx's Theory of History: A Defence* (Princeton University Press, 1978) ISBN 0-691-07068-7
- Collier, Andrew. *Marx* (Oneworld, 2004)
- Draper, Hal, *Karl Marx's Theory of Revolution* (4 volumes) Monthly Review Press
- Duncan, Ronald and Wilson, Colin. (editors) *Marx Refuted*, (Bath, UK, 1987) ISBN 0-906798-71-X
- Eagleton, Terry. *Why Marx Was Right* (New Haven & London: Yale University Press, 2011).
- Fine, Ben. *Marx's Capital.* 5th ed. London: Pluto, 2010.
- Foster, John Bellamy. *Marx's Ecology: Materialism and Nature.* New York: Monthly Review Press, 2000.

- Gould, Stephen Jay. *A Darwinian Gentleman at Marx's Funeral – E. Ray Lankester*[183], Page 1, Find Articles.com[184] (1999)
- Harvey, David. *A Companion to Marx's Capital.* London: Verso, 2010.
- Harvey, David. *The Limits of Capital.* London: Verso, 2006.
- Henry, Michel. *Marx I* and *Marx II.* 1976
- Holt, Justin P. *The Social Thought of Karl Marx.* Sage, 2015.
- Iggers, Georg G. "Historiography: From Scientific Objectivity to the Postmodern Challenge."(Wesleyan University Press, 1997, 2005)
- Kołakowski, Leszek. *Main Currents of Marxism* Oxford: Clarendon Press, OUP, 1978
- Little, Daniel. *The Scientific Marx*, (University of Minnesota Press, 1986) ISBN 0-8166-1505-5
- Mandel, Ernest. *Marxist Economic Theory.* New York: Monthly Review Press, 1970.
- Mandel, Ernest. *The Formation of the Economic Thought of Karl Marx.* New York: Monthly Review Press, 1977.
- Mészáros, István. *Marx's Theory of Alienation* (The Merlin Press, 1970)
- Miller, Richard W. *Analyzing Marx: Morality, Power, and History.* Princeton, N.J: Princeton University Press, 1984.
- Postone, Moishe. *Time, Labour, and Social Domination: A Reinterpretation of Marx's Critical Theory.* Cambridge [England]: Cambridge University Press, 1993.
- Rothbard, Murray. *An Austrian Perspective on the History of Economic Thought Volume II: Classical Economics* (Edward Elgar Publishing Ltd., 1995) ISBN 0-945466-48-X
- Saad-Filho, Alfredo. *The Value of Marx: Political Economy for Contemporary Capitalism.* London: Routledge, 2002.
- Schmidt, Alfred. *The Concept of Nature in Marx.* London: NLB, 1971.
- Seigel, J. E. (1973). "Marx's Early Development: Vocation, Rebellion and Realism". *The Journal of Interdisciplinary History.* 3 (3): 475–508. JSTOR 202551[185].
- Seigel, Jerrold. *Marx's fate: the shape of a life* (Princeton University Press, 1978) ISBN 0-271-00935-7
- Strathern, Paul. "Marx in 90 Minutes", (Ivan R. Dee, 2001)
- Thomas, Paul. *Karl Marx and the Anarchists.* London: Routledge & Kegan Paul, 1980.
- Uno, Kozo. *Principles of Political Economy. Theory of a Purely Capitalist Society*, Brighton, Sussex: Harvester; Atlantic Highlands, N.J.: Humanities, 1980.
- Vianello, F. [1989], "Effective Demand and the Rate of Profits: Some Thoughts on Marx, Kalecki and Sraffa", in: Sebastiani, M. (ed.), *Kalecki's Relevance Today*, London, Macmillan, ISBN 978-03-12-02411-6.

- Wendling, Amy. *Karl Marx on Technology and Alienation* (Palgrave Macmillan, 2009)
- Wheen, Francis. *Marx's Das Kapital*, (Atlantic Books, 2006) ISBN 1-84354-400-8
- Wilson, Edmund. *To the Finland Station: A Study in the Writing and Acting of History*, Garden City, NY: Doubleday, 1940

Fiction works

- Barker, Jason. *Marx Returns*, Winchester, UK: Zero Books, 2018, ISBN 9781785356605.

Medical articles

- Shuster, Sam (2008). "The nature and consequence of Karl Marx's skin disease". *British Journal of Dermatology*. **158** (1): 071106220718011–???. doi: 10.1111/j.1365-2133.2007.08282.x[186]. PMID 17986303[187].

External links

- Works by Karl Marx[188] at Project Gutenberg
- Works by or about Karl Marx[189] at Internet Archive
- Works by Karl Marx[190] at LibriVox (public domain audiobooks) ◀»
- Works by Karl Marx[191] (in German) at Zeno.org
- Karl Marx[192] at *Encyclopædia Britannica*
- Zalta, Edward N. (ed.). "Karl Marx"[193]. *Stanford Encyclopedia of Philosophy*.
- Marxists.org[194], homepage of the Marxists Internet Archive
- Institute of Marxism-Leninism of the Communist Party of the Soviet Union (1989). *Karl Marx: a Biography*[195] (4 ed.). Moscow: Progress Publishers.
- Krader, Lawrence, ed. (1974). *The Ethnological Notebooks of Karl Marx*[196] (PDF) (2 ed.). Assen: Van Gorcum.
- Archive of Karl Marx / Friedrich Engels Papers[197] at the International Institute of Social History
- The *Collected Works* of Marx and Engels, in English translation and in 50 volumes, are published in London by Lawrence & Wishart and in New York by International Publishers. (These volumes were at one time put online by the Marxists Internet Archive, until the original publishers objected on copyright grounds: "Marx/Engels Collected Works"[198]. *Marxists Internet Archive*. Retrieved 3 March 2018.) They are available online and searchable, for purchase or through subscribing libraries, in the

" Social Theory[199]" collection published by Alexander Street Press[200] in collaboration with the University of Chicago.
- Marx[201], BBC Radio 4 discussion with Anthony Grayling, Francis Wheen & Gareth Stedman Jones (*In Our Time*, 14 July 2005)
- Newspaper clippings about Karl Marx[202] in the 20th Century Press Archives of the German National Library of Economics (ZBW)

Articles and entries

- Dead Labour: Marx and Lenin Reconsidered[203] by Paul Craig Roberts
- Hegel, Marx, Engels, and the Origins of Marxism[204], by David North
- *In Praise of Marx*[205] Terry Eagleton synopsising his *Why Marx was right* chronicle.com 10 April 2011.
- *Karl Marx: An Overview of his Biographies*, by Angelo Segrillo[181]
- Karl Marx: Did he get it all Right?[206] by Philip Collins, *The Times*, 21 October 2008
- *Karl Marx*, Ernest Mandel[207]
- Liberalism, Marxism and The State[208], by Ralph Raico
- Marx, Mao and mathematics: the politics of infinitesimals[209], by Joseph Dauben
- Marxism and Ethics[210] from *International Socialism* Paul Blackledge (2008)
- Marxmyths.org Various essays on misinterpretations of Marx[211]
- Portraits of Karl Marx[212] (International Institute of Social History)
- Paul Dorn, The Paris Commune and Marx' Theory of Revolution[213]
- *Karl Marx (1818–1883)*[214]. *The Concise Encyclopedia of Economics*. Library of Economics and Liberty (2nd ed.). Liberty Fund. 2008.
- Marx's Revenge: How Class Struggle Is Shaping the World[215]. *TIME*, 25 March 2013.
- Marx Was Right: Five Surprising Ways Karl Marx Predicted 2014[216]. *Rolling Stone*, 30 January 2014.
- Karl Marx Was Right[217]. Chris Hedges for *Truthdig*, 31 May 2015.

<indicator name="good-star"> ⊕ </indicator>

Influences on Karl Marx

Influences on Karl Marx

Influences on Karl Marx are generally thought to have been derived from three sources: German idealist philosophy, French socialism and English and Scottish political economy.Wikipedia:Citation needed

German philosophy

Immanuel Kant

Immanuel Kant is believed to have had the greatest influence of any philosopher of modern times. Kantian philosophy was the basis on which the structure of Marxism was built—particularly as it was developed by Georg Wilhelm Friedrich Hegel. Hegel's dialectical method, which was taken up by Karl Marx, was an extension of the method of reasoning by "antinomies" that Kant used.

Georg Wilhelm Friedrich Hegel

By the time of his death, Hegel was the most prominent philosopher in Germany. His views were widely taught and his students were highly regarded. His followers soon divided into right-wing and left-wing Hegelians. Theologically and politically, the right-wing Hegelians offered a conservative interpretation of his work. They emphasized the compatibility between Hegel's philosophy and Christianity. Politically, they were orthodox. The left-wing Hegelians eventually moved to an atheistic position. In politics, many of them became revolutionaries. This historically important left-wing group included Ludwig Feuerbach, Bruno Bauer, Friedrich Engels and Marx himself. They were often referred to as the Young Hegelians.

Marx's view of history, which came to be called historical materialism, is certainly influenced by Hegel's claim that reality (and history) should be viewed

dialectically. Hegel believed that the direction of human history is characterized in the movement from the fragmentary toward the complete and the real
(which was also a movement towards greater and greater rationality). Sometimes, Hegel explained that this progressive unfolding of "the Absolute" involves gradual, evolutionary accretion, but at other times requires discontin-
uous, revolutionary leaps—episodal upheavals against the existing *status quo*.
For example, Hegel strongly opposed slavery in the United States during his
lifetime and envisioned a time when Christian nations would radically eliminate it from their civilization.

While Marx accepted this broad conception of history, Hegel was an idealist
and Marx sought to rewrite dialectics in materialist terms. He summarized the
materialistic aspect of his theory of history in the 1859 preface to *A Contribution to the Critique of Political Economy*:

> *In the social production of their existence, men inevitably enter into def-
> inite relations, which are independent of their will, namely relations of
> production appropriate to a given stage in the development of their mate-
> rial forces of production. The totality of these relations of production con-
> stitutes the economic structure of society, the real foundation, on which
> arises a legal and political superstructure and to which correspond def-
> inite forms of social consciousness. The mode of production of material
> life conditions the general process of social, political and intellectual life.
> It is not the consciousness of men that determines their existence, but their
> social existence that determines their consciousness.*

In this brief popularization of his ideas, Marx emphasized that social development sprang from the inherent contradictions within material life and the social
superstructure. This notion is often understood as a simple historical narrative:
primitive communism had developed into slave states. Slave states had developed into feudal societies. Those societies in turn became capitalist states and
those states would be overthrown by the self-conscious portion of their working class, or proletariat, creating the conditions for socialism and ultimately
a higher form of communism than that with which the whole process began.
Marx illustrated his ideas most prominently by the development of capitalism
from feudalism and by the prediction of the development of communism from
capitalism.

Ludwig Feuerbach

Ludwig Feuerbach was a German philosopher and anthropologist. Feuerbach
proposed that people should interpret social and political thought as their foundation and their material needs. He held that an individual is the product of
their environment and that the whole consciousness of a person is the result

of the interaction of sensory organs and the external world. Marx and Engels saw in Feuerbach's emphasis on people and human needs a movement toward a materialistic interpretation of society. In *The Essence of Christianity* (1841), Feuerbach argued that God is really a creation of man and that the qualities people attribute to God are really qualities of humanity. Accordingly, Marx argued that it is the material world that is real and that our ideas of it are consequences, not causes, of the world. Thus, like Hegel and other philosophers, Marx distinguished between appearances and reality. However, he did not believe that the material world hides from us the "real" world of the ideal; on the contrary, he thought that historically and socially specific ideology prevented people from seeing the material conditions of their lives clearly.

What distinguished Marx from Feuerbach was his view of Feuerbach's humanism as excessively abstract and so no less ahistorical and idealist than what it purported to replace, namely the reified notion of God found in institutional Christianity that legitimized the repressive power of the Prussian state. Instead, Marx aspired to give ontological priority to what he called the "real life process" of real human beings as he and Engels said in *The German Ideology* (1846):

> In direct contrast to German philosophy, which descends from heaven to earth, here we ascend from earth to heaven. That is to say, we do not set out from what men say, imagine, conceive, nor from men as narrated, thought of, imagined, conceived, in order to arrive at men in the flesh. We set out from real, active men, and on the basis of their real life process we demonstrate the development of the ideological reflexes and echoes of this life process. The phantoms formed in the human brain are also, necessarily, sublimates of their material life process, which is empirically verifiable and bound to material premises. Morality, religion, metaphysics, all the rest of ideology and their corresponding forms of consciousness, thus no longer retain the semblance of independence. They have no history, no development; but men, developing their material production and their material intercourse, alter, along with this, their real existence, their thinking, and the products of their thinking. Life is not determined by consciousness, but consciousness by life.

In his *Theses on Feuerbach* (1844), he also writes that "the philosophers have only interpreted the world, in various ways, the point is to change it". This opposition between firstly various subjective interpretations given by philosophers, which may be in a sense compared with *Weltanschauung* designed to legitimize the current state of affairs; and secondly, the effective transformation of the world through praxis, which combines theory and practice in a materialist way, is what distinguishes Marxist philosophers from the rest of philosophers. Indeed, Marx's break with German idealism involves a new definition of philosophy as Louis Althusser, founder of structural Marxism in the 1960s, would define it as "class struggle in theory". Marx's movement away from university philosophy and towards the workers' movement is thus inextricably linked to his rupture with his earlier writings, which pushed Marxist commentators to speak of a "young Marx" and a "mature Marx", although the nature of this cut poses problems. A year before the Revolutions of 1848, Marx and Engels thus wrote *The Communist Manifesto*, which was prepared to an imminent revolution and ended with the famous cry: "Proletarians of all countries, unite!". However, Marx's thought changed again following Louis-Napoleon Bonaparte's 2 December 1851 coup, which put an end to the French Second Republic and created the Second Empire which would last until the 1870 Franco-Prussian War. Marx thereby modified his theory of alienation exposed in the *Economic and Philosophical Manuscripts of 1844* and would latter arrive to his theory of commodity fetishism, exposed in the first chapter of the first book of *Das Kapital* (1867). This abandonment of the early theory of alienation would be amply discussed, several Marxist theorists, including Marxist humanists such as the Praxis School, would return to it. Others such as Althusser would claim that the "epistemological break" between the "young Marx" and the "mature Marx" was such that no comparisons could be done between both works, marking a shift to a "scientific theory" of society.

Rupture with German idealism and the Young Hegelians

Marx did not study directly with Hegel, but after Hegel's death he studied under one of Hegel's pupils, Bruno Bauer, a leader of the circle of Young Hegelians to whom Marx attached himself. However, Marx and Engels came to disagree with Bauer and the rest of the Young Hegelians about socialism and also about the usage of Hegel's dialectic. From 1841, the young Marx progressively broke away from German idealism and the Young Hegelians. Along with Engels, who observed the Chartist movement in the United Kingdom, he cut away with the environment in which he grew up and encountered the proletariat in France and Germany.

He then wrote a scathing criticism of the Young Hegelians in two books, *The Holy Family* (1845) and *The German Ideology* in which he criticized not only Bauer, but also Max Stirner's *The Ego and Its Own* (1844), considered as one of the founding book of individualist anarchism. Stirner claimed that all ideals were inherently alienating and that replacing God by the humanity—as did Ludwig Feuerbach in *The Essence of Christianity*—was not sufficient. According to Stirner, any ideals, God, humanity, the nation, or even the revolution alienated "the Ego". Marx also criticized Pierre-Joseph Proudhon, who had become famous with his cry "Property is theft!", in *The Poverty of Philosophy* (1845).

Marx's early writings are thus a response towards Hegel, German idealism and a break with the rest of the Young Hegelians. Marx "stood Hegel on his head" in his own view of his role by turning the idealistic dialectic into a materialistic one, in proposing that material circumstances shape ideas instead of the other way around. In this, Marx was following the lead of Feuerbach. His theory of alienation, developed in the *Economic and Philosophical Manuscripts of 1844* (published in 1932), inspired itself from Feuerbach's critique of the alienation of man in God through the objectivation of all his inherent characteristics (thus man projected on God all qualities which are in fact man's own quality which defines the "human nature"). However, Marx also criticized Feuerbach for being insufficiently materialistic—as Stirner himself had point out—and explained that the alienation described by the Young Hegelians was in fact the result of the structure of the economy itself. Furthermore, he criticized Feuerbach's conception of human nature in his sixth thesis on Feuerbach as an abstract "kind" which incarnated itself in each singular individual: "Feuerbach resolves the essence of religion into the essence of man (*menschliche Wesen*, human nature). But the essence of man is no abstraction inherent in each single individual. In reality, it is the ensemble of the social relations". Thereupon, instead of founding itself on the singular, concrete individual subject as did classic philosophy, including contractualism (Thomas Hobbes, John Locke and Jean-Jacques Rousseau), but also political economy, Marx began with the totality of social relations: labour, language and all which constitute our human existence. He claimed that individualism was an essence the result of commodity fetishism or alienation. Although some critics have claimed that meant that Marx enforced a strict social determinism which destroyed the possibility of free will, Marx's philosophy in no way can be reduced to such determinism as his own personal trajectory makes clear.

In 1844–1845, when Marx was starting to settle his account with Hegel and the Young Hegelians in his writings, he critiqued the Young Hegelians for limiting the horizon of their critique to religion and not taking up the critique of the state and civil society as paramount. Indeed, by the look of Marx's writings in that period (most famous of which is the *Economic and Philosophical Manuscripts of 1844*, a text that most explicitly elaborated his theory of alienation), Marx's thinking could have taken at least three possible courses: the study of law, religion and the state; the study of natural philosophy; and the study of political economy. He chose the last as the predominant focus of his studies for the rest of his life, largely on account of his previous experience as the editor of the newspaper *Rheinische Zeitung* on whose pages he fought for freedom of expression against Prussian censorship and made a rather idealist, legal defense for the Moselle peasants' customary right of collecting wood in the forest (this right was at the point of being criminalized and privatized by the state). It was Marx's inability to penetrate beneath the legal and polemical surface of the latter issue to its materialist, economic and social roots that prompted him to critically study political economy.

English and Scottish political economy

Political economy predates the 20th century division of the two disciplines of politics and economics, treating social relations and economic relations as interwoven. Marx built on and critiqued the most well-known political economists of his day, the British classical political economists.

Adam Smith and David Ricardo

From Adam Smith came the idea that the grounds of property is labour. Marx critiqued Smith and David Ricardo for not realizing that their economic concepts reflected specifically capitalist institutions, not innate natural properties of human society; and therefore could not be applied unchanged to all societies. He proposed a systematic correlation between labour-values and money prices. He claimed that the source of profits under capitalism is value added by workers not paid out in wages. This mechanism operated through the distinction between "labour power", which workers freely exchanged for their wages; and "labour", over which asset-holding capitalists thereby gained control.

This practical and theoretical distinction was Marx's primary insight and allowed him to develop the concept of "surplus value", which distinguished his works from that of Smith and Ricardo. Workers create enough value during a short period of the working day to pay their wages for that day (necessary labour), yet they continue to work for several more hours and continue to create value (surplus labour). This value is not returned to them, but appropriated by the capitalists (the bourgeoisie). Thus, it is not the capitalist ruling class that creates wealth, but the workers; the capitalists then appropriating this wealth to themselves. Some of Marx's insights were seen in a rudimentary form by the Ricardian socialist school).[218,219] He developed this theory of exploitation in *Das Capital*, a "dialectical" investigation into the forms value relations take.

Marx's theory of business cycles; of economic growth and development, especially in two sector models; and of the declining rate of profit, or crisis theory are other important elements of Marx's political economy. Marx later made tentative movements towards econometric investigations of his ideas, but the necessary statistical techniques of national accounting only emerged in the following century. In any case, it has proved difficult to adapt Marx's economic concepts, which refer to social relations, to measurable aggregated stocks and flows. In recent decades, a loose "quantitative" school of Marxist economists has emerged. While it may be impossible to find exact measures of Marx's variables from price data, approximations of basic trends are possible.

French socialism

Jean-Jacques Rousseau

Rousseau was one of the first modern writers to seriously attack the institution of private property and therefore is sometimes considered a forebear of modern socialism and communism, though Marx rarely mentions Rousseau in his writings. He argued that the goal of government should be to secure freedom, equality and justice for all within the state, regardless of the will of the majority. From Rousseau came the idea of egalitarian democracy.

Charles Fourier and Henri de Saint-Simon

In 1833, France was experiencing a number of social problems arising out of the Industrial Revolution. A number of sweeping plans of reform were developed by thinkers on the left. Among the more grandiose were the plans of Charles Fourier and the followers of Henri de Saint-Simon. Fourier wanted to replace modern cities with utopian communities while the Saint-Simonians advocated directing the economy by manipulating credit. Although these programs did not have much support, they did expand the political and social imagination of their contemporaries, including Marx.

Pierre-Joseph Proudhon

Proudhon participated in the February 1848 uprising and the composition of what he termed "the first republican proclamation" of the new republic. However, he had misgivings about the new government because it was pursuing political reform at the expense of the socio-economic reform, which Proudhon considered basic. Proudhon published his own perspective for reform, *Solution du problème social*, in which he laid out a program of mutual financial cooperation among workers. He believed this would transfer control of economic relations from capitalists and financiers to workers. It was Proudhon's book *What Is Property?* that convinced the young Marx that private property should be abolished.

In one of his first works, *The Holy Family*, Marx said: "Not only does Proudhon write in the interest of the proletarians, he is himself a proletarian, an ouvrier. His work is a scientific manifesto of the French proletariat". However, Marx disagreed with Proudhon's anarchism and later published vicious criticisms of Proudhon. Marx wrote *The Poverty of Philosophy* as a refutation of Proudhon's *The Philosophy of Poverty* (1847). In his socialism, Proudhon was followed by Mikhail Bakunin. After Bakunin's death, his libertarian socialism diverged into anarcho-communism and collectivist anarchism, with notable proponents such as Peter Kropotkin and Joseph Déjacque.

Other influences

Friedrich Engels

Marx's revision of Hegelianism was also influenced by Engels' 1845 book, *The Condition of the Working Class in England*, which led Marx to conceive of the historical dialectic in terms of class conflict and to see the modern working class as the most progressive force for revolution. Thereafter, Marx and Engels worked together for the rest of Marx's life so that the collected works of Marx and Engels are generally published together, almost as if the output of one person. Important publications, such as *The German Ideology* and *The Communist Manifesto*, were joint efforts. Engels says that "I cannot deny that both before and during my 40 years' collaboration with Marx I had a certain independent share in laying the foundation of the theory, and more particularly in its elaboration". However, he adds: <templatestyles src="Template:Quote/styles.css"/>

> But the greater part of its leading basic principles, especially in the realm of economics and history, and, above all, their final trenchant formulation, belong to Marx. What I contributed — at any rate with the exception of my work in a few special fields — Marx could very well have done without me. What Marx accomplished I would not have achieved. Marx stood higher, saw further, and took a wider and quicker view than all the rest of us. Marx was a genius; we others were at best talented. Without him the theory would not be by far what it is today. It therefore rightly bears his name.(Frederick Engels, Ludwig Feuerbach and the End of Classical German Philosophy Part 4: Marx)

Charles Darwin

In late November 1859, Engels acquired one of the first 1,250 copies of Charles Darwin's *The Origin of Species* and then he sent a letter to Marx telling: "Darwin, by the way, whom I'm just reading now, is absolutely splendid". The following year, Marx wrote back to his colleague telling that this book contained the natural-history foundation of the historical materialism viewpoint:[220,221] <templatestyles src="Template:Quote/styles.css"/>

> These last four weeks, I have read all sorts of things. Among others, Darwin's book on natural selection. Although it is developed in the crude

English style, this is the book which contains the basis on natural history for our view.

—*Karl Marx, 19 December 1860*[222,223]

Next month, Marx wrote to his friend Ferdinand Lassalle: <templatestyles src="Template:Quote/styles.css"/>

Darwin's work is most important and suits my purpose in that it provides a basis in natural science for the historical class struggle.

—*Karl Marx, 16 January 1861*[224]

By June 1862, Marx had already read *The Origin of Species* again, finding a connection between Thomas Robert Malthus's work and Darwin's ideas: <templatestyles src="Template:Quote/styles.css"/>

I am amused at Darwin, into whom I looked again, when he says that he applies the "Malthusian" theory also to plants and animals.

—*Karl Marx in a letter to Friedrich Engels, 18 June 1862*[225]

In 1863, he quoted Darwin again within his *Theories of Surplus Value* (2:121), saying: "In his splendid work, Darwin did not realize that by discovering the 'geometrical progression' in the animal and plant kingdom, he overthrew Malthus theory".[226]

Having read about darwinian evolution along with Marx, German communist Wilhelm Liebknecht later said that "when Darwin drew the conclusions from his research work and brought them to the knowledge of the public, we spoke of nothing else for months but Darwin and the enormous significance of his scientific discoveries".[227] Historian Richard Weikart points out that Marx had started to attend "a series of lectures by Thomas Henry Huxley on evolution".[228]

In August 1866, Marx referred to Pierre Trémaux's *Origine et transformations de l'homme et des autres êtres* (1865) in another letter to Engels as "a very important advance over Darwin".[229] He went further to claim that "in its historical and political application", the book was "much more important and copious than Darwin".[230]

Although there is no mention of Darwin in *The Communist Manifesto* (published eleven years prior to *The OIrigin of Species*), Marx includes two explicit references to Darwin and evolution in the second edition of *Das Kapital*, in two footnotes where he relates Darwin's theory to his opinion about production and technology development. In the Volume I, Chapter 14: "The Detail Labourer and his implements", Section 2, he referred to Darwin's *Origin of*

Species as an "epoch-making work"[231,232] while in Chapter 15, Section I he took on the comparison of organs of plants to animals and tools.[233]

In a book review of the first volume of *Das Kapital*, Engels wrote that Marx was "simply striving to establish the same gradual process of transformation demonstrated by Darwin in natural history as a law in the social field". In this line of thought, several authors such as William F. O'Neill, have seen that "Marx describes history as a social Darwinist 'survival of the fittest' dominated by the conflict between different social classes" and moving to a future in which social conflict will ultimately disappear in a 'classless society'"[234,235] while some Marxists try to dissociate Marx from social Darwinism.

Nonetheless, it is evident that Marx had a strong liking for Darwin's theory and a clear influence on his thought. Furthermore, when the second German edition of *Das Capital*, was published (two years after the publication of Darwin's *Descent of Man, and Selection in Relation to Sex*), Marx sent Darwin a copy of his book with the following words:[236] <templatestyles src="Template:Quote/styles.css"/>

> *Mr. Charles Darwin*
> *On the part of his sincere admirer*
> *Karl Marx*
>
> *—London, 16 June 1873*[237,238]

Darwin wrote back to Marx in October, thanking him for having sent his work and saying "I believe that we both earnestly desire the extension of knowledge".[239]

According to scholar Paul Heyer, "Marx believed that Darwin provided a materialistic perspective compatible with his own", although being applied in another context.[240] In his book *Darwin in Russian Thought* (1989), Alexander Vucinich claims that "Engels gave Marx credit for extending Darwin's theory to the study of the inner dynamics and change in human society".[241]

Classical materialism

Marx was influenced by classical materialism, especially Epicurus (to whom Marx dedicated his thesis, "Difference of Natural Philosophy Between Democritus and Epicurus", 1841) for his materialism and theory of clinamen which opened up a realm of liberty.

Lewis H. Morgan

Marx drew on Lewis H. Morgan and his social evolution theory. He wrote a collection of notebooks from his reading of Morgan, but they are regarded as being quite obscure and only available in scholarly editions.

Marx's theory of human nature

Marx's theory of human nature

Part of a series on
Marxism

- 🏴 Socialism portal
- ⚒ Communism portal
- 📖 Philosophy portal

- v
- t
- e[242]

Some MarxistsWikipedia:Manual of Style/Words to watch#Unsupported attributions posit what they deem to be **Karl Marx's theory of human nature**,

which they accord an important place in his critique of capitalism, his conception of communism, and his 'materialist conception of history'. Marx, however, does not refer to human nature as such, but to *Gattungswesen*, which
is generally translated as 'species-being' or 'species-essence'. According to a
note from the young Marx in the *Manuscripts of 1844*, the term is derived
from Ludwig Feuerbach's philosophy, in which it refers both to the nature of
each human and of humanity as a whole.

However, in the sixth *Theses on Feuerbach* (1845), Marx criticizes the traditional conception of human nature as a species which incarnates itself in each
individual, instead arguing that the conception of human nature is formed by
the totality of social relations. Thus, the whole of human nature is not understood, as in classical idealist philosophy, as permanent and universal: the
species-being is always determined in a specific social and historical formation,
with some aspects being biological.

The sixth thesis on Feuerbach and the determina-
tion of human nature by social relations

The sixth of the *Theses on Feuerbach*, written in 1845, provided an early discussion by Marx of the concept of human nature. It states:

> *Feuerbach resolves the essence of religion into the essence of man
> [menschliches Wesen = 'human nature']. But the essence of man is no
> abstraction inherent in each single individual. In reality, it is the ensem-
> ble of the social relations. Feuerbach, who does not enter upon a criticism
> of this real essence is hence obliged:*
>
> > *1. To abstract from the historical process and to define the religious
> > sentiment regarded by itself, and to presuppose an abstract — isolated
> > - human individual.*
> >
> > *2. The essence therefore can by him only be regarded as 'species',
> > as an inner 'dumb' generality which unites many individuals only in a
> > natural way.*

*Thus, Marx appears to say that human nature is no more than what is
made by the 'social relations'. Norman Geras's Marx and Human Nature
(1983), however, offers an argument against this position.*[243] *In outline,
Geras shows that, while the social relations are held to 'determine' the
nature of people, they are not the only such determinant. However, Marx
makes statements where he specifically refers to a human nature which is
more than what is conditioned by the circumstances of one's life. In Capital, in a footnote critiquing utilitarianism, he says that utilitarians must*

reckon with 'human nature in general, and then with human nature as modified in each historical epoch'. Marx is arguing against an abstract conception of human nature, offering instead an account rooted in sensuous life. While he is quite explicit that '[a]s individuals express their life, so they are. Hence what individuals are depends on the material conditions of their production', he also believes that human nature will condition (against the background of the productive forces and relations of production, the way in which individuals express their life. History involves 'a continuous transformation of human nature', though this does not mean that every aspect of human nature is wholly variable; what is transformed need not be wholly transformed.

Marx did criticise the tendency to 'transform into eternal laws of nature and of reason, the social forms springing from your present mode of production and form of property'.[244] For this reason, he would likely have wanted to criticise certain aspects of some accounts of human nature. Some people believe, for example, that humans are naturally selfish - Immanuel Kant and Thomas Hobbes, for example. (Both Hobbes and Kant thought that it was necessary to constrain our human nature in order to achieve a good society - Kant thought we should use rationality, Hobbes thought we should use the force of the state - Marx, as we shall see, thought that the good society was one which allows our human nature its full expression.) Most Marxists will argue that this view is an ideological illusion and the effect of commodity fetishism: the fact that people act selfishly is held to be a product of scarcity and capitalism, not an immutable human characteristic. For confirmation of this view, we can see how, in The Holy Family Marx argues that capitalists are not motivated by any essential viciousness, but by the drive toward the bare 'semblance of a human existence'. (Marx says 'semblance' because he believes that capitalists are as alienated from their human nature under capitalism as the proletariat, even though their basic needs are better met.)

Needs and drives

In the *1844 Manuscripts* the young Marx wrote:

Man is directly a natural being. As a natural being and as a living natural being he is on the one hand endowed with natural powers, vital powers – he is an active natural being. These forces exist in him as tendencies and abilities – as instincts. On the other hand, as a natural, corporeal, sensuous objective being he is a suffering, conditioned and limited creature, like animals and plants. That is to say, the objects of his instincts exist outside him, as objects independent of him; yet these objects are objects that he needs – essential objects, indispensable to the manifestation and confirmation of his essential powers.

In the *Grundrisse* Marx says his nature is a 'totality of needs and drives'. In *The German Ideology* he uses the formulation: 'their *needs*, consequently their nature'. We can see then, that from Marx's early writing to his later work, he conceives of human nature as composed of 'tendencies', 'drives', 'essential powers', and 'instincts' to act in order to satisfy 'needs' for external objectives. For Marx then, an explanation of human nature is an explanation of the needs of humans, together with the assertion that they will act to fulfill those needs. (c.f. *The German Ideology*, chapter 3). Norman Geras gives a schedule of some of the needs which Marx says are characteristic of humans:

...for other human beings, for sexual relations, for food, water, clothing, shelter, rest and, more generally, for circumstances that are conducive to health rather than disease. There is another one ... the need of people for a breadth and diversity of pursuit and hence of personal development, as Marx himself expresses these, 'all-round activity', 'all-round development of individuals', 'free development of individuals', 'the means of cultivating [one's] gifts in all directions', and so on.[245]

Marx says 'It is true that eating, drinking, and procreating, etc., are ... genuine human functions. However, when abstracted from other aspects of human activity, and turned into final and exclusive ends, they are animal.'[246]

Productive activity, the objects of humans and actualisation

Humans as free, purposive producers

In several passages throughout his work, Marx shows how he believes humans to be essentially different from other animals. 'Men can be distinguished from animals by consciousness, by religion or anything else you like. They themselves begin to distinguish themselves from animals as soon as they begin to produce their means of subsistence, a step which is conditioned by their physical organisation.' In this passage from *The German Ideology*, Marx alludes to one difference: that humans produce their physical environments. But do not a few other animals also produce aspects of their environment as well? The previous year, Marx had already acknowledged:

It is true that animals also produce. They build nests and dwellings, like the bee, the beaver, the ant, etc. But they produce only their own immediate needs or those of their young; they produce only when immediate physical need compels them to do so, while man produces even when he is free from physical need and truly produces only in freedom from such need; they produce only themselves, while man reproduces the whole of nature; their products belong immediately to their physical bodies, while man freely confronts his own product. Animals produce only according to the standards and needs of the species to which they belong, while man is capable of producing according to the standards of every species and of applying to each object its inherent standard; hence, man also produces in accordance with the laws of beauty.

In the same work, Marx writes:

The animal is immediately one with its life activity. It is not distinct from that activity; it is that activity. Man makes his life activity itself an object of his will and consciousness. He has conscious life activity. It is not a determination with which he directly merges. Conscious life activity directly distinguishes man from animal life activity. Only because of that is he a species-being. Or, rather, he is a conscious being – i.e., his own life is an object for him, only because he is a species-being. Only because of that is his activity free activity. Estranged labour reverses the relationship so that man, just because he is a conscious being, makes his life activity, his essential being, a mere means for his existence.

Also in the segment on Estranged Labour:

Man is a species-being, not only because he practically and theoretically makes the species – both his own and those of other things – his object, but also – and this is simply another way of saying the same thing – because he looks upon himself as the present, living species, because he looks upon himself as a universal and therefore free being.

More than twenty years later, in *Capital*, he came to muse on a similar subject:

A spider conducts operations that resemble those of a weaver, and a bee puts to shame many an architect in the construction of her cells. But what distinguishes the worst architect from the best of bees is this, that the architect raises his structure in imagination before he erects it in reality. At the end of every labour-process, we get a result that already existed in the imagination of the labourer at its commencement. He not only effects a change of form in the material on which he works, but he also realises a purpose of his own that gives the law to his *modus operandi*, and to which he must subordinate his will. And this subordination is no mere momentary act.

From these passages we can observe something of Marx's beliefs about humans. That they characteristically produce their environments, and that they would do so, even were they not under the burden of 'physical need' - indeed, they will produce the 'whole of [their] nature', and may even create 'in accordance with the laws of beauty'. Perhaps most importantly, though, their creativity, their production is *purposive* and *planned*. Humans, then, make plans for their future activity, and attempt to exercise their production (even lives) according to them. Perhaps most importantly, and most cryptically, Marx says that humans make both their 'life activity' and 'species' the 'object' of their will. They relate to their life activity, and are not simply identical with it. Michel Foucault's definition of biopolitics as the moment when "man begins to take itself as a conscious object of elaboration" may be compared to Marx's definition hereby exposed.

Life and the species as the objects of humans

To say that A is the object of some subject B, means that B (specified as an agent) acts upon A in some respect. Thus if 'the proletariat smashes the state' then 'the state' is the object of the proletariat (the subject), in respect of smashing. It is similar to saying that A is the *objective* of B, though A could be a whole sphere of concern and not a closely defined aim. In this context, what does it mean to say that humans make their 'species' and their 'lives' their 'object'? It's worth noting that Marx's use of the word 'object' can imply that these are things which humans produces, or makes, just as they might produce a material object. If this inference is correct, then those things that Marx says about human production above, also apply to the production of human life, by humans. And simultaneously, 'As individuals express their life, so they are. What they are, therefore, coincides with their production, both with what they produce and with how they produce. The nature of individuals thus depends on the material conditions determining their production.'

To make one's life one's object is therefore to treat one's life as something that is under one's control. To raise in imagination plans for one's future and present, and to have a stake in being able to fulfill those plans. To be able to live a life of this character is to achieve 'self-activity' (actualisation), which Marx believes will only become possible after communism has replaced capitalism. 'Only at this stage does self-activity coincide with material life, which corresponds to the development of individuals into complete individuals and the casting-off of all natural limitations. The transformation of labour into self-activity corresponds to the transformation of the earlier limited intercourse into the intercourse of individuals as such'.

What is involved in making one's species one's object is more complicated (see Allen Wood 2004, pp. 16–21). In one sense, it emphasises the essentially social character of humans, and their need to live in a community of the species. In others, it seems to emphasise that we attempt to make our lives expressions of our species-essence; further that we have goals concerning what becomes of the species in general. The idea covers much of the same territory as 'making one's life one's object': it concerns self-consciousness, purposive activity, and so forth.

Humans as *homo faber*?

It is often said that Marx conceived of humans as *homo faber*, referring to Benjamin Franklin's definition of 'man as the tool-making animal' - that is, as 'man, the maker', though he never used the term himself. Above, we indicated that one of Marx's central contentions about humans was that they were differentiated by the manner in which they produce and that thus, somehow, production was one of humans' essential activities. In this context, it is worth noting that Marx does not always address 'labour' or 'work' in such glowing terms. He says that communism 'does away with labour'. Furthermore, 'If it is desired to strike a mortal blow at private property, one must attack it not only as a material state of affairs, but also as activity, as labour. It is one of the greatest misapprehensions to speak of free, human, social labour, of labour without private property. "Labour" by its very nature is unfree, unhuman, unsocial activity, determined by private property and creating private property.' Under Capitalism '[t]he capitalist functions only as capital personified, capital as a person, just as the worker only functions as the personification of labour, which belongs to him as torment, as exertion'.

It is generally held that Marx's view was that productive activity is an essential human activity, and can be rewarding when pursued freely. Marx's use of the words 'work' and 'labour' in the section above may be unequivocally negative; but this was not always the case, and is most strongly found in his early writing. However, Marx was always clear that under capitalism, labour was something inhuman, and dehumanising. 'labour is external to the worker – i.e., does not belong to his essential being; that he, therefore, does not confirm himself in his work, but denies himself, feels miserable and not happy, does not develop free mental and physical energy, but mortifies his flesh and ruins his mind'. While under communism, 'In the individual expression of my life I would have directly created your expression of your life, and therefore in my individual activity I would have directly confirmed and realised my true nature, my human nature, my communal nature'.

Human nature and historical materialism

Marx's theory of history attempts to describe the way in which humans change their environments and (in dialectical relation) their environments change them as well. That is:

Not only do the objective conditions change in the act of reproduction, e.g. the village becomes a town, the wilderness a cleared field etc., but the producers change, too, in that they bring out new qualities in themselves, develop themselves in production, transform themselves, develop new powers and ideas, new modes of intercourse, new needs and new language.

Further Marx sets out his 'materialist conception of history' in opposition to 'idealist' conceptions of history; that of Georg Wilhelm Friedrich Hegel, for instance. 'The first premise of all human history is, of course, the existence of living human individuals. Thus the first fact to be established is the physical organisation of these individuals and their consequent relation to the rest of nature.' Thus 'History does nothing, it "possesses no immense wealth", it "wages no battles". It is man, real, living man who does all that, who possesses and fights; "history" is not, as it were, a person apart, using man as a means to achieve its own aims; history is nothing but the activity of man pursuing his aims'. So we can see that, even before we begin to consider the precise character of human nature, 'real, living' humans, 'the activity of man pursuing his aims' is the very building block of Marx's theory of history. Humans act upon the world, changing it and themselves; and in doing so they 'make history'. However, even beyond this, human nature plays two key roles. In the first place, it is part of the explanation for the growth of the productive forces, which Marx conceives of as the driving force of history. Secondly, the particular needs and drives of humans explain the class antagonism which is generated under capitalism.

Human nature and the expansion of the productive forces

It has been held by several writers that it is Marx's conception of human nature which explains the 'development thesis' (Cohen, 1978) concerning the expansion of the productive forces, which according to Marx, is itself the fundamental driving force of history. If true, this would make his account of human nature perhaps the most fundamental aspect of his work. Geras writes, (1983, pp. 107–108, italics in original) *historical materialism itself, this whole distinctive approach to society that originates with Marx, rests squarely upon the idea of a human nature.* It highlights that specific nexus of universal needs and capacities which explains the human productive process and man's organized transformation of the material environment; which process and transformation it treats in turn as the basis both of the social order and of historical change.' G.A. Cohen (1988, p. 84): 'The tendency's autonomy is just its independence of social structure, its rootedness in fundamental material facts of human nature and the human situation.' Allen Wood (2004, p. 75): 'Historical progress consists fundamentally in the growth of people's abilities to shape and control the world about them. This is the most basic way in which they develop and express their human essence' (see also, the quotation from Allen Wood above).

In his article *Reconsidering Historical Materialism*, however, Cohen gives an argument to the effect that human nature cannot be the premise on which the plausibility of the expansion of the productive forces is grounded.

> 'Production in the historical anthropology is not identical with production in the theory of history. According to the anthropology, people flourish in the cultivation and exercise of their manifold powers, and are especially productive - which in *this* instance means creative - in the condition of freedom conferred by material plenty. But, in the production of interest to the theory of history, people produce not freely but because they have to, since nature does not otherwise supply their wants; and the development in history of the productive power of *man* (that is, of man as such, of man as a species) occurs at the expense of the creative capacity of the *men* who are agents and victims of that development.' (p. 166 in ed. Callinicos, 1989)

The implication of this is that hence 'one might ... imagine two kinds of creature, one whose essence it was to create and the other not, undergoing similarly toilsome histories because of similarly adverse circumstances. In one case, but not the other, the toil would be a self-alienating exercise of essential powers' (p. 170). Hence, 'historical materialism and Marxist philosophical anthropology are independent of, though also consistent with, each other' (p. 174, see especially sections 10 and 11). The problem is this: it seems as though the motivation most people have for the work they do isn't the exercise of their creative capacity; on the contrary, labour is alienated by definition in the capitalist system based on salary, and people only do it because they have to. They go to work not to express their human nature but to find theirs means of subsistence. So in that case, why do the productive forces grow - does human nature have anything to do with it? The answer to this question is a difficult one, and a closer consideration of the arguments in the literature is necessary for a full answer than can be given in this article. However, it is worth bearing in mind that Cohen had previously been committed to the strict view that human nature (and other 'asocial premises') were *sufficient* for the development of the productive forces - it could be that they are only one *necessary* constituent. It is also worth considering that by 1988 (see quotation above), he appears to consider that the problem is resolved.

Some needs are far more important than others. In *The German Ideology* Marx writes that 'life involves before everything else eating and drinking, a habitation, clothing and many other things'. All those other aspects of human nature which he discusses (such as 'self-activity') are therefore subordinate to the priority given to these. Marx makes explicit his view that humans develop new needs to replace old: 'the satisfaction of the first need (the action of satisfying, and the instrument of satisfaction which has been acquired) leads to new needs'.

Human nature, Marx's ethical thought and alienation

Geras says of Marx's work that: 'Whatever else it is, theory and socio-historical explanation, and scientific as it may be, that work is a moral indictment resting on the conception of essential human needs, an ethical standpoint, in other words, in which a view of human nature is involved' (1983, pp. 83–84).

Alienation

For the main article on this topic, see Marx's theory of alienation

Alienation, for Marx, is the estrangement of humans from aspects of their human nature. Since - as we have seen - human nature consists in a particular set of vital drives and tendencies, whose exercise constitutes flourishing, alienation is a condition wherein these drives and tendencies are stunted. For essential powers, alienation substitutes disempowerment; for making one's own life one's object, one's life becoming an object of capital. Marx believes that alienation will be a feature of all society before communism. The opposite of, alienation is 'actualisation' or 'self-activity' - the activity of the self, controlled by and for the self.Wikipedia:Citation needed

Gerald Cohen's criticism

One important criticism of Marx's 'philosophical anthropology' (i.e. his conception of humans) is offered by Gerald Cohen, the leader of Analytical Marxism, in *Reconsidering Historical Materialism* (in ed. Callinicos, 1989). Cohen claims: 'Marxist philosophical anthropology is one sided. Its conception of human nature and human good overlooks the need for self-identity than which nothing is more essentially human.' (p. 173, see especially sections 6 and 7). The consequence of this is held to be that 'Marx and his followers have underestimated the importance of phenomena, such as religion and nationalism, which satisfy the need for self-identity. (Section 8.)' (p. 173). Cohen describes what he sees as the origins of Marx's alleged neglect: 'In his anti-Hegelian, Feuerbachian affirmation of the radical objectivity of matter, Marx focused on the relationship of the subject to an object which is in no way subject, and, as time went on, he came to neglect the subject's relationship to itself, and that aspect of the subject's relationship to others which is a mediated (that is, indirect), form of relationship to itself' (p. 155).

Cohen believes that people are driven, typically, not to create identity, but to preserve that which they have in virtue, for example, of 'nationality, or race, or religion, or some slice or amalgam thereof' (pp. 156–159). Cohen does not claim that 'Marx denied that there is a need for self-definition, but [instead claims that] he failed to give the truth due emphasis' (p. 155). Nor does Cohen say that the sort of self-understanding that can be found through religion etc. is accurate (p. 158). Of nationalism, he says 'identifications [can] take benign, harmless, and catastrophically malignant forms' (p. 157) and does not believe 'that the state is a good medium for the embodiment of nationality' (p. 164).

References and further reading

All the quotations from Marx in this article have used the translation employed by the Marxists Internet Archive. This means that you can follow the external reference links, and then search on that page using your browser's search function for some part of the text of the quotation in order to ascertain its context.

Primary texts

The two texts in which Marx most directly discusses human nature are the *Comments on James Mill*[247] and the piece on *Estranged Labour*[248] in the *Economic and Philosophical Manuscripts of 1844* (published in 1932). Both of these pieces date from 1844, and as such were written by the young Marx; some analysts (Louis Althusser, etc.) assert that work from this period differs markedly in its ideas from the later work.

Accounts prior to 1978

In certain aspects, the views of many earlier writers on this topic are generally believed to have been superseded. Nevertheless, here is a selection of the best writing prior to 1978. Much of it addresses human nature through the strongly related concept of alienation:

- Erich Fromm, *Marx's Concept of Man. With a Translation of Marx's Economic and Philosophical Manuscripts by T. B. Bottomore*, (1961).
- Eugene Kamenka, *The Ethical Foundations of Marxism* (1962). The entire book can be read online[249].
- István Mészáros, *Marx's Theory of Alienation* (1970). Sections can be read online[250].
- Bertell Ollman, *Alienation: Marx's Conception of Man in Capitalist Society* (1971). Many chapters, including some directly relevant to human nature, can be read online[251].
- John Plamenatz, *Karl Marx's Philosophy of Man*, (1975).

Recent general accounts

- *Marx and Human Nature: Refutation of a Legend* by Norman Geras (1983) is a concise argument against the view that Marx did not believe there was something such as human nature, in particular the confusion surrounding the sixth of the *Theses on Feuerbach*.
- Part I of *Karl Marx* by Allen Wood provides a highly readable survey of the evidence concerning what Marx thought of human nature and his concept of alienation. See especially chapter 2. The preface to the second edition (2004) of Wood's book can be read online[252]. The first edition was published in 1983.
- *Marx and the Missing Link: Human Nature* by W. Peter Archibald (1989).
- *Marxism and Human Nature*[253] by Sean Sayers (1998).
- *The young Karl Marx: German philosophy, Modern politics, and human flourishing* by David Leopold (2007) See Chapter 4 for close reading of Marx's 1843 texts, relating human nature to human emancipation.[254]

The debate over human nature and historical materialism

- Pages 150–160 (i.e. chapter 6, section 4) of G.A. Cohen's seminal *Karl Marx's Theory of History* (*KMTH*) (1978) contain an account of the relation of human nature to historical materialism. Cohen argues that the former is necessary to explain the development of the productive forces, which Marx holds to drive history.
- This basic view is endorsed by Geras (1983) and Woods (1983, 2004).
- The view, however, was criticised by Erik Olin Wright and Andrew Levine in an article entitled *Rationality and Class Struggle*, first published in the *New Left Review*. It can be found as chapter 1 of *Marxist Theory* (ed. Alex Callinicos, 1989).
- It was also criticised by Joshua Cohen, in a review of *KMTH* in the *Journal of Philosophy*.
- G.A. Cohen draws out some difficulties with his own presentation in *KMTH* in the article *Reconsidering Historical Materialism*. (First published 1983 in *Marxism: NOMOS XXVI*, ed. Chapman and Pennock; now available in *Marxist Theory* ed. Alex Callinicos, 1989; and in *History, Labour, and Freedom*, G.A. Cohen, 1988). The article's contentions (for a five-point summary, see Callinicos pp. 173–4) concern the connection of Marx's historical materialism to his 'philosophical anthropology' - basically, his conception of human nature.
- Chapter 5 of G.A. Cohen's *History, Labour and Freedom* (1988) is entitled *Human Nature and Social Change in the Marxist Conception of History* and is co-authored by Cohen and Will Kymlicka. (First published 1988 in the Journal of Philosophy.) The purpose of the chapter is to defend Cohen's contention in his *KMTH* that there is an *autonomous* tendency of the productive forces to develop, where 'autonomous' means 'independent of particular social relations'. The text is a response to the criticisms of J. Cohen, Levine and Wright. That is, G.A. Cohen and Kymlicka seek to show that there are no grounds for an *a priori* denial' of the claim that 'extra-social features of human nature and the human situation operate powerfully enough to generate an historical tendency capable of overcoming recalcitrant social structures' (p. 106). There may be thought to be a tension between the claims of this article and those of *Reconsidering Historical Materialism*.

Labour theory of value

Labor theory of value

The **labor theory of value** (**LTV**) is a theory of value that argues that the economic value of a good or service is determined by the total amount of "socially necessary labor" required to produce it, rather than by the use or pleasure its owner gets from it (demand) and its scarcity value (supply). It does not say that the value of a commodity is determined by the actual amount of labor contained in it, but the average amount needed to produce it. This is called "socially necessary labor".

LTV is usually associated with Marxian economics, although it is also used in the theories of earlier classical liberal economists such as Adam Smith and David Ricardo and later also in anarchist economics. Smith saw the price of a commodity in terms of the labor that the purchaser must expend to buy it, which embodies the concept of how much labor a commodity, a tool for example, can save the purchaser. The LTV is central to Marxist theory, which holds that the working class is exploited under capitalism, and dissociates price and value. Marx never referred to his own theory of value as a "labour theory of value" even once.[255] Modern economics tends to deny the need for a LTV, concentrating instead on a theory of price determined by supply and demand.

Definitions of value and labor

When speaking in terms of a labor theory of value, "value," without any qualifying adjective should theoretically refer to the amount of labor necessary to produce a marketable commodity, including the labor necessary to develop any real capital used in the production. Both David Ricardo[256] and Karl Marx tried to quantify and embody all labor components in order to develop a theory of the real price, or natural price of a commodity.[257] The labor theory of value as presented by Adam Smith did not require the quantification of past labor, nor did it deal with the labor needed to create the tools (capital) that might be used in producing a commodity. Smith's theory of value was very similar to the later utility theories in that Smith proclaimed that a commodity was worth whatever labor it would command in others (value in trade) or whatever labor it would "save" the self (value in use), or both. However, this "value" is subject to supply and demand at a particular time:

> The real price of every thing, what every thing really costs to the man who wants to acquire it, is the toil and trouble of acquiring it. What every thing is really worth to the man who has acquired it, and who wants to dispose of it or exchange it for something else, is the toil and trouble which it can save to himself, and which it can impose upon other people. (Wealth of Nations Book 1, chapter V)

Smith's theory of price (which for many is the same as value) has nothing to do with the past labor spent in producing a commodity. It speaks only of the labor that can be "commanded" or "saved" at present. If there is no use for a buggy whip, then the item is economically worthless in trade or in use, regardless of all the labor spent in creating it.

Distinctions of economically pertinent labor

Value "in use" is the usefulness of this commodity, its utility. A classical paradox often comes up when considering this type of value. In the words of Adam Smith:

> The word value, it is to be observed, has two different meanings, and sometimes expresses the utility of some particular object, and sometimes the power of purchasing other goods which the possession of that object conveys. The one may be called "value in use"; the other, "value in exchange." The things which have the greatest value in use have frequently little or no value in exchange; and, on the contrary, those which have the greatest value in exchange have frequently little or no value in use. Nothing is more useful than water: but it will purchase scarce anything; scarce anything can be had in exchange for it. A diamond, on the contrary, has scarce any value in use; but a very great quantity of other goods may frequently be had in exchange for it (Wealth of Nations Book 1, chapter IV).

Value "in exchange" is the relative proportion with which this commodity exchanges for another commodity (in other words, its price in the case of money). It is relative to labor as explained by Adam Smith:

> The value of any commodity, [...] to the person who possesses it, and who means not to use or consume it himself, but to exchange it for other commodities, is equal to the quantity of labour which it enables him to

> purchase or command. *Labour, therefore, is the real measure of the ex-changeable value of all commodities (Wealth of Nations Book 1, chapter V).*

Value (without qualification) is the labor embodied in a commodity under a given structure of production. Marx defined the value of the commodity by the third definition. In his terms, value is the 'socially necessary abstract labor' embodied in a commodity. To David Ricardo and other classical economists, this definition serves as a measure of "real cost", "absolute value", or a "measure of value" invariable under changes in distribution and technology.[258]

Ricardo, other classical economists and Marx began their expositions with the assumption that value in exchange was equal to or proportional to this labor value. They thought this was a good assumption from which to explore the dynamics of development in capitalist societies. Other supporters of the labor theory of value used the word "value" in the second sense to represent "exchange value".[259]

LTV and the labor process

Since the term "value" is understood in the LTV as denoting something created by labor, and its "magnitude" as something proportional to the quantity of labor performed, it is important to explain how the labor process both preserves value and adds new value in the commodities it creates.[260]

The value of a commodity increases in proportion to the duration and intensity of labor performed on average for its production. Part of what the LTV means by "socially necessary" is that the value only increases in proportion to this labor as it is performed with average skill and average productivity. So though workers may labor with greater skill or more productivity than others, these more skillful and more productive workers thus produce more value through the production of greater quantities of the finished commodity. Each unit still bears the same value as all the others of the same class of commodity. By working sloppily, unskilled workers may drag down the average skill of labor, thus increasing the average labor time necessary for the production of each unit commodity. But these unskillful workers cannot hope to sell the result of their labor process at a higher price (as opposed to value) simply because they have spent more time than other workers producing the same kind of commodities.

However, production not only involves labor, but also certain means of labor: tools, materials, power plants and so on. These means of labor—also known as means of production—are often the product of another labor process as well. So the labor process inevitably involves these means of production that already enter the process with a certain amount of value. Labor also requires other means of production that are not produced with labor and therefore bear no value: such as sunlight, air, uncultivated land, unextracted minerals, etc. While useful, even crucial to the production process, these bring no value to that process. In terms of means of production resulting from another labor process, LTV treats the magnitude of value of these produced means of production as constant throughout the labor process. Due to the constancy of their value, these means of production are referred to, in this light, as constant capital.

Consider for example workers who take coffee beans, use a roaster to roast them, and then use a brewer to brew and dispense a fresh cup of coffee. In performing this labor, these workers add value to the coffee beans and water that comprise the material ingredients of a cup of coffee. The worker also transfers the value of constant capital—the value of the beans; some specific depreciated value of the roaster and the brewer; and the value of the cup—to the value of the final cup of coffee. Again, on average the worker can transfer no more than the value of these means of labor previously possessed to the finished cup of coffee[261] So the value of coffee produced in a day equals the sum of both the value of the means of labor—this constant capital—and the value newly added by the worker in proportion to the duration and intensity of their work.

Often this is expressed mathematically as:

$$c + L = W,$$

where

- c is the constant capital of materials used in a period plus the depreciated portion of tools and plant used in the process. (A period is typically a day, week, year, or a single turnover: meaning the time required to complete one batch of coffee, for example.)
- L is the quantity of labor time (average skill and productivity) performed in producing the finished commodities during the period
- W is the value (or think "worth") of the product of the period (w comes from the German word for value: *wert*)

Note: if the product resulting from the labor process is homogeneous (all similar in quality and traits, for example, all cups of coffee) then the value of the period's product can be divided by the total number of items (use-values or v_u) produced to derive the unit value of each item. $w_i = \frac{W}{\sum v_u}$ where $\sum v_u$ is the total items produced.

The LTV further divides the value added during the period of production, L , into two parts. The first part is the portion of the process when the workers add value equivalent to the wages they are paid. For example, if the period in question is one week and these workers collectively are paid \$1,000, then the time necessary to add \$1,000 to—while preserving the value of—constant capital is considered the necessary labor portion of the period (or week): denoted NL . The remaining period is considered the surplus labor portion of the week: or SL . The value used to purchase labor-power, for example the \$1,000 paid in wages to these workers for the week, is called variable capital (v). This is because in contrast to the constant capital expended on means of production, variable capital can add value in the labor process. The amount it adds depends on the duration, intensity, productivity and skill of the labor-power purchased: in this sense the buyer of labor-power has purchased a commodity of variable use. Finally, the value added during the portion of the period when surplus labor is performed is called surplus value (s). From the variables defined above, we find two other common expressions for the value produced during a given period:

$$c + v + s = W$$

and

$$c + NL + SL = W$$

The first form of the equation expresses the value resulting from production, focusing on the costs $c + v$ and the surplus value appropriated in the process of production, s . The second form of the equation focuses on the value of production in terms of the values added by the labor performed during the process $NL + SL$.

Relation between values and prices

One issue facing the LTV is the relationship between value quantities on one hand and prices on the other. If a commodity's value is not the same as its price, and therefore the magnitudes of each likely differ, then what is the relation between the two, if any? Various LTV schools of thought provide different answers to this question. For example, some argue that value in the sense of the amount of labor embodied in a good acts as a center of gravity for price.

However, most economists would say that cases where pricing is given as approximately equal to the value of the labour embodied, are in fact only special cases. In General Theory pricing most usually fluctuates. The standard formulation is that prices normally include a level of income for "capital" and "land". These incomes are known as "profit" and "rent" respectively. Yet

Marx made the point that value cannot be placed upon labour as a commodity, because capital is a constant, whereas profit is a variable, not an income; thus explaining the importance of profit in relation to pricing variables.[262]

In Book 1, chapter VI, Adam Smith writes:

> *The real value of all the different component parts of price, it must be observed, is measured by the quantity of labour which they can, each of them, purchase or command. Labour measures the value not only of that part of price which resolves itself into labour, but of that which resolves itself into rent, and of that which resolves itself into profit.*

The final sentence explains how Smith sees value of a product as relative to labor of buyer or consumer, as opposite to Marx who sees the value of a product being proportional to labor of laborer or producer. And we value things, price them, based on how much labor we can avoid or command, and we can command labor not only in a simple way but also by trading things for a profit.

The demonstration of the relation between commodities' unit values and their respective prices is known in Marxian terminology as the transformation problem or the transformation of values into prices of production. The transformation problem has probably generated the greatest bulk of debate about the LTV. The problem with transformation is to find an algorithm where the magnitude of value added by labor, in proportion to its duration and intensity, is sufficiently accounted for after this value is distributed through prices that reflect an equal rate of return on capital advanced. If there is an additional magnitude of value or a loss of value after transformation, then the relation between values (proportional to labor) and prices (proportional to total capital advanced) is incomplete. Various solutions and impossibility theorems have been offered for the transformation, but the debate has not reached any clear resolution.

LTV does not deny the role of supply and demand influencing price, since the price of a commodity is something other than its value. In *Value, Price and Profit* (1865), Karl Marx quotes Adam Smith and sums up:

> It suffices to say that if supply and demand equilibrate each other, the market prices of commodities will correspond with their natural prices, that is to say, with their values as determined by the respective quantities of labor required for their production.[263]

The LTV seeks to explain the level of this equilibrium. This could be explained by a *cost of production* argument—pointing out that all costs are ultimately labor costs, but this does not account for profit, and it is vulnerable to the charge of tautology in that it explains prices by prices.[264] Marx later called this "Smith's adding up theory of value".

Smith argues that labor values are the natural measure of exchange for direct producers like hunters and fishermen.[265] Marx, on the other hand, uses a measurement analogy, arguing that for commodities to be comparable they must have a common element or substance by which to measure them,[266] and that labor is a common substance of what Marx eventually calls *commodity-values*.

History

Origins

The labor theory of value has developed over many centuries. It had no single originator, but rather many different thinkers arrived at the same conclusion independently. Aristotle is claimed to hold to this view. Some writers trace its origin to Thomas Aquinas. In his *Summa Theologiae* (1265–1274) he expresses the view that "... value can, does and should increase in relation to the amount of labor which has been expended in the improvement of commodities." Scholars such as Joseph Schumpeter have cited Ibn Khaldun, who in his *Muqaddimah* (1377), described labor as the source of value, necessary for all earnings and capital accumulation. He argued that even if earning "results from something other than a craft, the value of the resulting profit and acquired (capital) must (also) include the value of the labor by which it was obtained. Without labor, it would not have been acquired." Scholars have also pointed to Sir William Petty's *Treatise of Taxes* of 1662[267] and to John Locke's labor theory of property, set out in the *Second Treatise on Government* (1689), which sees labor as the ultimate source of economic value. Karl Marx himself credited Benjamin Franklin in his 1729 essay entitled "A Modest Enquiry into the Nature and Necessity of a Paper Currency" as being "one of the first" to advance the theory.[268]

Adam Smith accepted the theory for pre-capitalist societies but saw a flaw in its application to contemporary capitalism. He pointed out that if the "labor embodied" in a product equaled the "labor commanded" (i.e. the amount of labor that could be purchased by selling it), then profit was impossible. David Ricardo (seconded by Marx) responded to this paradox by arguing that Smith had confused labor with wages. "Labor commanded", he argued, would always be more than the labor needed to sustain itself (wages). The value of labor, in this view, covered not just the value of wages (what Marx called the value of labor power), but the value of the entire product created by labor.[269]

Ricardo's theory was a predecessor of the modern theory that equilibrium prices are determined solely by production costs associated with Neo-Ricardianism.[270]

Based on the discrepancy between the wages of labor and the value of the product, the "Ricardian socialists"—Charles Hall, Thomas Hodgskin, John Gray, and John Francis Bray, and Percy Ravenstone[271]—applied Ricardo's theory to develop theories of exploitation.

Marx expanded on these ideas, arguing that workers work for a part of each day adding the value required to cover their wages, while the remainder of their labor is performed for the enrichment of the capitalist. The LTV and the accompanying theory of exploitation became central to his economic thought.

19th century American individualist anarchists based their economics on the LTV, with their particular interpretation of it being called "Cost the limit of price". They, as well as contemporary individualist anarchists in that tradition, hold that it is unethical to charge a higher price for a commodity than the amount of labor required to produce it. Hence, they propose that trade should be facilitated by using notes backed by labor.

Adam Smith and David Ricardo

Adam Smith held that, in a primitive society, the amount of labor put into producing a good determined its exchange value, with exchange value meaning in this case the amount of labor a good can purchase. However, according to Smith, in a more advanced society the market price is no longer proportional to labor cost since the value of the good now includes compensation for the owner of the means of production: "The whole produce of labour does not always belong to the labourer. He must in most cases share it with the owner of the stock which employs him."[272] "Nevertheless, the 'real value' of such a commodity produced in advanced society is measured by the labor which that commodity will command in exchange. ... But [Smith] disowns what is naturally thought of as the genuine classical labor theory of value, that labor-cost regulates market-value. This theory was Ricardo's, and really his alone."[273]

Classical economist David Ricardo's labor theory of value holds that the value of a good (how much of another good or service it exchanges for in the market) is proportional to how much labor was required to produce it, including the labor required to produce the raw materials and machinery used in the process. David Ricardo stated it as, "The value of a commodity, or the quantity of any other commodity for which it will exchange, depends on the relative quantity of labour which is necessary for its production, and not as the greater or less compensation which is paid for that labour." (Ricardo 1817) In this connection Ricardo seeks to differentiate the quantity of labour necessary to produce a commodity from the wages paid to the laborers for its production. However, Ricardo was troubled with some deviations in prices from proportionality with the labor required to produce them.[274] For example, he said "I cannot get over the difficulty of the wine, which is kept in the cellar for three or four years [i.e., while constantly increasing in exchange value], or that of the oak tree, which perhaps originally had not 2 s. expended on it in the way of labour, and yet comes to be worth £100." (Quoted in Whitaker) Of course, a capitalist economy stabilizes this discrepancy until the value added to aged wine is equal to the cost of storage. If anyone can hold onto a bottle for four years and become rich, that would make it hard to find freshly corked wine. There is also the theory that adding to the price of a luxury product increases its exchange-value by mere prestige.

The labor theory as an explanation for value contrasts with the subjective theory of value, which says that value of a good is not determined by how much labor was put into it but by its usefulness in satisfying a want and its scarcity. Ricardo's labor theory of value is not a normative theory, as are some later forms of the labor theory, such as claims that it is *immoral* for an individual to be paid less for his labor than the total revenue that comes from the sales of all the goods he produces.

It is arguable to what extent these classical theorists held the labor theory of value as it is commonly defined.[275,276,277] For instance, David Ricardo theorized that prices are determined by the amount of labor but found exceptions for which the labor theory could not account. In a letter, he wrote: "I am not satisfied with the explanation I have given of the principles which regulate value." Adam Smith theorized that the labor theory of value holds true only in the "early and rude state of society" but not in a modern economy where owners of capital are compensated by profit. As a result, "Smith ends up making little use of a labor theory of value."[278]

Anarchism

Pierre Joseph Proudhon's mutualism[279] and American individualist anarchists such as Josiah Warren, Lysander Spooner and Benjamin Tucker[280] adopted the liberal Labor Theory of Value of classical economics and used it to criticize capitalism while favoring a non-capitalist market system.[281]

Warren is widely regarded as the first American anarchist,[282,283] and the four-page weekly paper he edited during 1833, *The Peaceful Revolutionist*, was the first anarchist periodical published.[284] Cost the limit of price was a maxim coined by Warren, indicating a (prescriptive) version of the labor theory of value. Warren maintained that the just compensation for labor (or for its product) could only be an equivalent amount of labor (or a product embodying an equivalent amount).[285] Thus, profit, rent, and interest were considered unjust economic arrangements.[286] In keeping with the tradition of Adam Smith's *The Wealth of Nations*,[287] the "cost" of labor is considered to be the subjective cost; i.e., the amount of suffering involved in it. He put his theories to the test by establishing an experimental "labor for labor store" called the Cincinnati Time Store at the corner of 5th and Elm Streets in what is now downtown

Sample Labor Note

Figure 20: *Sample labor for labor note for the Cincinnati Time Store. Scanned from Equitable Commerce (1846) by Josiah Warren*

Cincinnati, where trade was facilitated by notes backed by a promise to perform labor. "All the goods offered for sale in Warren's store were offered at the same price the merchant himself had paid for them, plus a small surcharge, in the neighborhood of 4 to 7 percent, to cover store overhead." The store stayed open for three years; after it closed, Warren could pursue establishing colonies based on Mutualism. These included "Utopia" and "Modern Times". Warren said that Stephen Pearl Andrews' *The Science of Society*, published in 1852, was the most lucid and complete exposition of Warren's own theories.[288]

Mutualism is an economic theory and anarchist school of thought that advocates a society where each person might possess a means of production, either individually or collectively, with trade representing equivalent amounts of labor in the free market. Integral to the scheme was the establishment of a mutual-credit bank that would lend to producers at a minimal interest rate, just high enough to cover administration.[289] Mutualism is based on a labor theory of value that holds that when labor or its product is sold, in exchange, it ought to receive goods or services embodying "the amount of labor necessary to produce an article of exactly similar and equal utility".[290] Mutualism originated from the writings of philosopher Pierre-Joseph Proudhon.

Collectivist anarchism as defended by Mikhail Bakunin defended a form of labor theory of value when it advocated a system where "all necessaries for production are owned in common by the labour groups and the free communes ... based on the distribution of goods according to the labour contributed".

Karl Marx

Contrary to popular belief Marx never used the term "Labor theory of value" in any of his works but used the term Law of value,[292] Marx opposed "ascribing a supernatural creative power to labor", arguing as such:

> Labor is not the source of all wealth. Nature is just as much a source of use values (and it is surely of such that material wealth consists!) as labor, which is itself only the manifestation of a force of nature, human labor power.[293]

Here, Marx was distinguishing between exchange value (the subject of the LTV) and use value. Marx used the concept of "socially necessary labor time" to introduce a social perspective distinct from his predecessors and neoclassical economics. Whereas most economists start with the individual's perspective, Marx started with the perspective of society *as a whole*. "Social production" involves a complicated and interconnected division of labor of a wide variety of people who depend on each other for their survival and prosperity. "Abstract" labor refers to a characteristic of commodity-producing labor that is shared by all different kinds of heterogeneous (concrete) types of labor. That is, the concept abstracts from the *particular* characteristics of all of the labor and is akin to average labor.

"Socially necessary" labor refers to the quantity required to produce a commodity "in a given state of society, under certain social average conditions or production, with a given social average intensity, and average skill of the labor employed".[294] That is, the value of a product is determined more by societal standards than by individual conditions. This explains why technological breakthroughs lower the price of commodities and put less advanced producers out of business. Finally, it is not labor per se which creates value, but labor power sold by free wage workers to capitalists. Another distinction to be made is that between productive and unproductive labor. Only wage workers of productive sectors of the economy produce value.[295]

Criticisms

The Marxist labor theory of value has been criticised on several counts. Some argueWikipedia:Citation needed that it predicts that profits will be higher in labor-intensive industries than in capital-intensive industries, which would be contradicted by measured empirical data inherent in quantitative analysis. Even if Marx has never 'mechanically' simplified the matter in these terms, as capital itself is product of past labour, thus, the 'general tendency of falling profit' does not concern or invalidate the labour origin of value, present in both live and dead labour (capital)(cf chapter 1 and 24 of Das Kapital). This is sometimes referred to as the "Great Contradiction".[296] In volume 3 of Capital, Marx explains why profits are not distributed according to which industries are the most labor-intensive and why this is consistent with his theory. Whether or not this is consistent with the labor theory of value as presented in volume 1 has been a topic of debate. According to Marx, surplus value is extracted by the capitalist class as a whole and then distributed according to the amount of total capital, not the just variable component. In the example given earlier, of making a cup of coffee, the constant capital involved in production is the coffee beans themselves, and the variable capital is the value added by the coffee maker. The value added by the coffee maker is dependent on its technological capabilities, and the coffee maker can only add so much total value to cups of coffee over its lifespan. The amount of value added to the product is thus the amortization of the value of the coffeemaker. We can also note that not all products have equal proportions of value added by amortized capital. Capital intensive industries such as finance may have a large contribution of capital, while labor-intensive industries like traditional agriculture would have a relatively small one.[297]

The theory can also be sometimes found in non-Marxist traditions.[298] For instance mutualist anarchist theorist Kevin Carson's *Studies in Mutualist Political Economy* opens with an attempt to integrate marginalist critiques into the labor theory of value.[299]

Some Post-Keynesian economists have been highly critical of the labor theory of value. Joan Robinson, who herself was considered an expert on the writings of Karl Marx, wrote that the labor theory of value was largely a tautology and "a typical example of the way metaphysical ideas operate".[300]

Others have argued that the labor theory of value, especially as it arises in the work of Karl Marx, is due to a failure to recognize the fundamentally dialectical nature of how human beings attribute value to objects. Pilkington writes that value is attributed to objects based on our desire for them and that this desire is always inter-subjective and socially determined. He writes the following:

> [V]alue is attributed to objects due to our desire for them. This desire, in turn, is inter-subjective. We desire to gain [a] medal or to capture [an] enemy flag [in battle] because it will win recognition in the eyes of our peers. [A] medal [or an enemy] flag are not valued for their objective properties, nor are they valued for the amount of labour embodied in them, rather they are desired for the symbolic positions they occupy in the inter-subjective network of desires.

Pilkington insists that this is an entirely different conception of value than the one we find in the marginalist theory found in many economics textbooks. He writes that "actors in marginalist analysis have self-contained preferences; they do not have inter-subjective desires".[301]

In ecological economics, the labor theory of value has been criticized, where it is argued that labor is in fact energy over time.[302] However, echoing Joan Robinson, Alf Hornborg, an environmental historian, argues that both the reliance on "energy theory of value" and "labor theory of value" are problematic as they propose that use-values (or material wealth) are more "real" than exchange-values (or cultural wealth)–yet, use-values are culturally determined.[303] For Hornborg, any Marxist argument that claims uneven wealth is due to the "exploitation" or "underpayment" of use-values is actually a tautological contradiction, since it must necessarily quantify "underpayment" in terms of exchange-value. The alternative would be to conceptualize unequal exchange as "an asymmetric net transfer of material inputs in production (e.g., embodied labor, energy, land, and water), rather than in terms of an underpayment of material inputs or an asymmetric transfer of 'value'".[304] In other words, uneven exchange is characterised by incommensurability, namely: the unequal transfer of material inputs; competing value-judgements of the worth of labor, fuel, and raw materials; differing availability of industrial technologies; and the off-loading of environmental burdens on those with less resources.[305]

A generalization

To resolve the above-mentioned contradiction of the theory with reality, some authors proposed to reconsider the role of production equipment (constant capital) in production of value, following hints in *Das Kapital*, where Marx described the functional role of machinery in production processes in Chapter XV (Machinery and Modern Industry) in the following words:

> *On a closer examination of the working machine proper, we find in it, as a general rule, though often, no doubt, under very altered forms, the apparatus and tools used by the handicraftsmen or manufacturing workman: with this difference that instead of being human implements, they are the implements of a mechanism, or mechanical implements (pp. 181–182). The machine proper is therefore a mechanism that, after being set in motion performs with its tools the same operations that were formerly done by the workman with similar tools. Whether the motive power is derived from man or from some other machine, makes no difference in this respect (p. 182). The implements of labour, in the form of machinery, necessitate the substitution of natural forces for human force, and the conscious application of science instead of rule of thumb (p. 188). After making allowance, both in the case of the machine and of the tool, for their average daily cost, that is, for the value they transmit to the product by their average daily wear and tear, and for their consumption of auxiliary substances such as oil, coal and so on, they each do their work gratuitously, just like the forces furnished by nature without the help of man (p. 189).*

These words state that one has to account, while interpreting production of value, that the workers' efforts in production of things are substituted with work of production equipment with due effect. Really, at substitution of labourer's work by forces of the nature, that is at substitution of efforts of people by work of external forces of the nature by means of the production equipment, work operates in a complex as workers' efforts plus work of the equipment. Thus, work of machines can be appreciated only so far as this work does what people wish, replacing their efforts and, consequently, a measure of value, certainly, can be the labourers' work only.

Further reading

- Bhaduri, Amit. 1969. "On the Significance of Recent Controversies on Capital Theory: A Marxian View." *Economic Journal*. 79(315) September: 532-539.
- von Böhm-Bawerk, Eugen *Karl Marx and the Close of His System* (Classic criticism of Marxist economic theory).

- G. A. Cohen 'The Labour Theory of Value and the Concept of Exploitation', in his *History Labour and Freedom*.
- Duncan, Colin A. M. 1996. *The Centrality of Agriculture: Between Humankind and The Rest of Nature*. Mc-Gill-Queen's University Press, Montreal.
- –2000 The Centrality of Agriculture: History, Ecology and Feasible Socialism. Socialist Register, pp. 187–205.
- –2004 Adam Smith's green vision and the future of global socialism. In Albritton, R; Shannon Bell; John R. Bell; and R. Westra [Eds.] *New Socialisms: Futures Beyond Globalization*. New York/London, Routledge. pp. ;90–104.
- Dussel, Enique (2002), "The four drafts of '"Capital"'"[306] (PDF), *Rethinking Marxism*, **13** (1): 10., doi: 10.1080/0893569011012415690[307], retrieved August 3, 2006
- Eldred, Michael (1984) *Critique of Competitive Freedom and the Bourgeois-Democratic State: Outline of a Form-analytic Extension of Marx's Uncompleted System*[308]. With an Appendix 'Value-form Analytic Reconstruction of the Capital-Analysis' by Michael Eldred, Marnie Hanlon, Lucia Kleiber and Mike Roth, Kurasje, Copenhagen. Emended, digitized edition 2010 with a new Preface, lxxiii + 466 pp. ISBN 87-87437-40-6, ISBN 978-87-87437-40-0.
- Ellerman, David P. (1992) Property & Contract in Economics: The Case for Economic Democracy. Blackwell. Chapters 4,5, and 13 critiques of LTV in favor of the labor theory of property.
- Engels, F. (1880). *Socialism: Utopian and Scientific*[309].
- Freeman, Alan: *Price, value and profit - a continuous, general treatment*. In: Alan Freeman, Guglielmo Carchedi (editors): *Marx and Non-equilibrium Economics*. Edward Elgar Publishing. Cheltenham, UK, Brookfield, US 1996. ISBN 978-1-85898-268-7.
- Hagendorf, Klaus: *The Labour Theory of Value. A Historical-Logical Analysis*[310]. Paris: EURODOS; 2008.
- Hagendorf, Klaus: *Labour Values and the Theory of the Firm. Part I: The Competitive Firm*[311]. Paris: EURODOS; 2009.
- Henderson, James M.; Quandt, Richard E. 1971: Microeconomic Theory - A Mathematical Approach. Second Edition/International Student Edition. McGraw-Hill Kogakusha, Ltd.
- Keen, Steven *Use, Value, and Exchange: The Misinterpretation of Marx*[312].
- Mason, Paul (2015). *PostCapitalism: A Guide to our Future*. Allen Lane. ISBN 978-1-84614-738-8.
- Marx, Karl (1867), Frederick Engels, ed., *Capital: Volume 1*[313], Samuel Moore and Edward Aveling, Marxist.org, ISBN 0-394-72657-X, retrieved

July 5, 2006 ([Internet edition: 1999] [1887 English edition]).

- Ormazabal, Kepa M. (2004). *Smith On Labour Value*[314] Bilbo, Biscay, Spain: University of the Basque Country Working Paper.
- Parrington, Vernon Louis. *The Autobiography of Benjamin Franklin*[315].
- Pokrovskii, Vladimir (2011). *Econodynamics. The Theory of Social Production.*[316] Springer, Dordrecht-Heidelberg-London-New York.
- Shaikh, Anwar (1998). "The Empirical Strength of the Labour Theory of Value" in *Conference Proceedings of Marxian Economics: A Centenary Appraisal*, Riccardo Bellofiore (ed.), Macmillan, London.
- Smith, Adam (1776), *An Inquiry into the Nature and Causes of the Wealth of Nations*[317], AdamSmith.org, ISBN 1-4043-0998-5, archived from the original[318] on September 27, 2007, retrieved August 3, 2006
- Vianello, F. [1987], "Labour theory of value", in: Eatwell, J. and Milgate, M. and Newman, P. (eds.): *The New Palgrave: A Dictionary of Economics*, Macmillan e Stockton, London e New York, ISBN 978-0-935859-10-2.
- Wolff, Jonathan (2003). " *Karl Marx*[319] in *Stanford Encyclopedia of Philosophy*.
- Wolff, Richard D., Bruce B. Roberts and Antonio Callari (1982), "Marx's (not Ricardo's) 'Transformation Problem': A Radical Reconceptualization", *History of Political Economy*, **14** (4): 564–582, doi: 10.1215/00182702-14-4-564[320].

The Communist Manifesto

The Communist Manifesto

The Communist Manifesto

First edition, in German

Author	Karl Marx and Friedrich Engels
Translator	Samuel Moore
Country	United Kingdom
Language	German
Publication date	late-February 1848

The Communist Manifesto (originally *Manifesto of the Communist Party*) is an 1848 political pamphlet by the German philosophers Karl Marx and Friedrich Engels. Commissioned by the Communist League and originally published in London (in German as *Manifest der Kommunistischen Partei*) just as the revolutions of 1848 began to erupt, the *Manifesto* was later recognised as one of the world's most influential political documents. It presents an analytical approach to the class struggle (historical and then-present) and the conflicts of capitalism and the capitalist mode of production, rather than a prediction of communism's potential future forms.

The Communist Manifesto summarises Marx and Engels' theories concerning the nature of society and politics, that in their own words, "The history of all hitherto existing society is the history of class struggles". It also briefly features their ideas for how the capitalist society of the time would eventually be replaced by socialism. Near the end of the Manifesto, the authors call for "forcible overthrow of all existing social conditions", which served as the justification for all communist revolutions around the world.

In 2013, *The Communist Manifesto* was registered to UNESCO's Memory of the World Programme with *Capital, Volume I*.[321]

Synopsis

The Communist Manifesto is divided into a preamble and four sections, the last of these a short conclusion. The introduction begins by proclaiming "A spectre is haunting Europe—the spectre of communism. All the powers of old Europe have entered into a holy alliance to exorcise this spectre". Pointing out that parties everywhere—including those in government and those in the opposition—have flung the "branding reproach of communism" at each other, the authors infer from this that the powers-that-be acknowledge communism to be a power in itself. Subsequently, the introduction exhorts Communists to openly publish their views and aims, to "meet this nursery tale of the spectre of communism with a manifesto of the party itself".

The first section of the *Manifesto*, "Bourgeois and Proletarians", elucidates the materialist conception of history, that "the history of all hitherto existing society is the history of class struggles". Societies have always taken the form of an oppressed majority exploited under the yoke of an oppressive minority. In capitalism, the industrial working class, or *proletariat*, engage in class struggle against the owners of the means of production, the *bourgeoisie*. As before, this struggle will end in a revolution that restructures society, or the "common ruin of the contending classes". The bourgeoisie, through the "constant revolutionising of production [and] uninterrupted disturbance of all social conditions" have emerged as the supreme class in society, displacing all the old powers of feudalism. The bourgeoisie constantly exploits the proletariat for its labour power, creating profit for themselves and accumulating capital. However, in doing so, the bourgeoisie serves as "its own grave-diggers"; the proletariat inevitably will become conscious of their own potential and rise to power through revolution, overthrowing the bourgeoisie.

"Proletarians and Communists", the second section, starts by stating the relationship of conscious communists to the rest of the working class. The communists' party will not oppose other working-class parties, but unlike them, it will express the general will and defend the common interests of the world's proletariat as a whole, independent of all nationalities. The section goes on to defend communism from various objections, including claims that it advocates "free love" or disincentivises people from working. The section ends by outlining a set of short-term demands—among them a progressive income tax; abolition of inheritances and private property; abolition of child labour; free public education; nationalisation of the means of transport and communication; centralisation of credit via a national bank; expansion of publicly owned etc.—the implementation of which would result in the precursor to a stateless and classless society.

The third section, "Socialist and Communist Literature", distinguishes communism from cther socialist doctrines prevalent at the time—these being broadly categorised as Reactionary Socialism; Conservative or Bourgeois Socialism; and Critical-Utopian Socialism and Communism. While the degree of reproach toward rival perspectives varies, all are dismissed for advocating reformism and failing to recognise the pre-eminent revolutionary role of the working class. "Position of the Communists in Relation to the Various Opposition Parties", the concluding section of the *Manifesto*, briefly discusses the communist position on struggles in specific countries in the mid-nineteenth century such as France, Switzerland, Poland, and Germany, this last being "on the eve of a bourgeois revolution", and predicts that a world revolution will soon follow. It ends by declaring an alliance with the social democrats, boldly supporting other communist revolutions, and calling for united international proletarian action—Working Men of All Countries, Unite!.

Writing

In spring 1847 Marx and Engels joined the League of the Just, who were quickly convinced by the duo's ideas of "critical communism". At its First Congress in 2–9 June, the League tasked Engels with drafting a "profession of faith", but such a document was later deemed inappropriate for an open, non-confrontational organisation. Engels nevertheless wrote the "Draft of a Communist Confession of Faith", detailing the League's programme. A few months later, in October, Engels arrived at the League's Paris branch to find that Moses Hess had written an inadequate manifesto for the group, now called the League of Communists. In Hess's absence, Engels severely criticised this manifesto, and convinced the rest of the League to entrust him with drafting a new one. This became the draft *Principles of Communism*, described as "less of a credo and more of an exam paper."

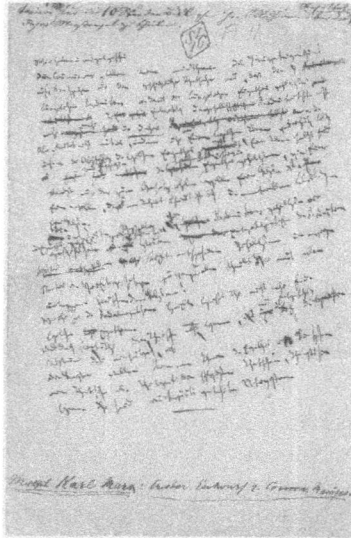

Figure 21: *Only surviving page from the first
draft of the Manifesto, handwritten by Marx*

On 23 November, just before the Communist League's Second Congress (29
November – 8 December 1847), Engels wrote to Marx, expressing his desire
to eschew the catechism format in favour of the manifesto, because he felt it
"must contain some history." On the 28th, Marx and Engels met at Ostend
in Belgium, and a few days later, gathered at the Soho, London headquarters
of the German Workers' Education Association to attend the Congress. Over
the next ten days, intense debate raged between League functionaries; Marx
eventually dominated the others and, overcoming "stiff and prolonged opposition", in Harold Laski's words, secured a majority for his programme. The
League thus unanimously adopted a far more combative resolution than that
at the First Congress in June. Marx (especially) and Engels were subsequently
commissioned to draw up a manifesto for the League.

Upon returning to Brussels, Marx engaged in "ceaseless procrastination", according to his biographer Francis Wheen. Working only intermittently on the
manifesto, he spent much of his time delivering lectures on political economy at the German Workers' Education Association, writing articles for the
Deutsche-Brüsseler-Zeitung, and giving a long speech on free trade. Following this, he even spent a week (17–26 January 1848) in Ghent to establish a
branch of the Democratic Association there. Subsequently, having not heard
from Marx for nearly two months, the Central Committee of the Communist

Figure 22: *A scene from the German March Revolution in Berlin, 1848*

League sent him an ultimatum on 24 or 26 January, demanding he submit the completed manuscript by 1 February. This imposition spurred Marx on, who struggled to work without a deadline, and he seems to have rushed to finish the job in time. (For evidence of this, historian Eric Hobsbawm points to the absence of rough drafts, only one page of which survives.)

In all, the *Manifesto* was written over 6–7 weeks. Although Engels is credited as co-writer, the final draft was penned exclusively by Marx. From the 26 January letter, Laski infers that even the League considered Marx to be the sole draftsman (and that he was merely their agent, imminently replaceable). Further, Engels himself wrote in 1883 that "The basic thought running through the *Manifesto* ... belongs solely and exclusively to Marx." Although Laski doesn't disagree, he suggests that Engels underplays his own contribution with characteristic modesty, and points out the "close resemblance between its substance and that of the [*Principles of Communism*]". Laski argues that while writing the *Manifesto*, Marx drew from the "joint stock of ideas" he developed with Engels, "a kind of intellectual bank account upon which either could draw freely."

Publication

Initial publication and obscurity, 1848–72

In late February 1848, the *Manifesto* was anonymously published by the Workers' Educational Association (*Communistischer Arbeiterbildungsverein*)

Figure 23: *Immediately after the Cologne Communist Trial of late 1852, the Communist League disbanded itself.*

at Bishopsgate in the City of London. Written in German, the 23-page pamphlet was titled *Manifest der kommunistischen Partei* and had a dark-green cover. It was reprinted three times and serialised in the *Deutsche Londoner Zeitung*, a newspaper for German *émigré*s. On 4 March, one day after the serialisation in the *Zeitung* began, Marx was expelled by Belgian police. Two weeks later, around 20 March, a thousand copies of the *Manifesto* reached Paris, and from there to Germany in early April. In April–May the text was corrected for printing and punctuation mistakes; Marx and Engels would use this 30-page version as the basis for future editions of the *Manifesto*.

Although the *Manifesto*'s prelude announced that it was "to be published in the English, French, German, Italian, Flemish and Danish languages", the initial printings were only in German. Polish and Danish translations soon followed the German original in London, and by the end of 1848, a Swedish translation was published with a new title—*The Voice of Communism: Declaration of the Communist Party*. In June–November 1850 the *Manifesto of the Communist Party* was published in English for the first time when George Julian Harney serialised Helen Macfarlane's translation in his Chartist magazine *The Red Republican*. (Her version begins, "A frightful hobgoblin stalks throughout Europe. We are haunted by a ghost, the ghost of Communism.")[322] For her translation, the Lancashire-based Macfarlane probably consulted Engels, who had abandoned his own English translation half way. Harney's introduction revealed the *Manifesto*'s hitherto-anonymous authors' identities for the first time.

Soon after the *Manifesto* was published, Paris erupted in revolution to over-throw King Louis Philippe. The *Manifesto* played no role in this; a French translation was not published in Paris until just before the working-class June Days Uprising was crushed. Its influence in the Europe-wide revolutions of 1848 was restricted to Germany, where the Cologne-based Communist League and its newspaper *Neue Rheinische Zeitung*, edited by Marx, played an impor-tant role. Within a year of its establishment, in May 1849, the *Zeitung* was suppressed; Marx was expelled from Germany and had to seek lifelong refuge in London. In 1851, members of the Communist League's central board were arrested by the Prussian police. At their trial in Cologne 18 months later in late 1852 they were sentenced to 3–6 years' imprisonment. For Engels, the revolution was "forced into the background by the reaction that began with the defeat of the Paris workers in June 1848, and was finally excommunicated 'by law' in the conviction of the Cologne Communists in November 1852".

After the defeat of the 1848 revolutions the *Manifesto* fell into obscurity, where it remained throughout the 1850s and 1860s. Hobsbawm says that by November 1850 the *Manifesto* "had become sufficiently scarce for Marx to think it worth reprinting section III ... in the last issue of his [short-lived] London magazine". Over the next two decades only a few new editions were published; these include an (unauthorised and occasionally inaccurate) 1869 Russian translation by Mikhail Bakunin in Geneva and an 1866 edition in Berlin—the first time the *Manifesto* was published in Germany. According to Hobsbawm, "By the middle 1860s virtually nothing that Marx had written in the past was any longer in print." However John Cowell-Stepney did pub-lish an abridged version in the *Social Economist* in August/September 1869, in time for the Basle Congress.

Rise, 1872–1917

In the early 1870s, the *Manifesto* and its authors experienced a revival in for-tunes. Hobsbawm identifies three reasons for this. The first is the leader-ship role Marx played in the International Workingmen's Association (aka the First International). Secondly, Marx also came into much prominence among socialists—and equal notoriety among the authorities—for his support of the Paris Commune of 1871, elucidated in *The Civil War in France*. Lastly, and perhaps most significantly in the popularisation of the *Manifesto*, was the trea-son trial of German Social Democratic Party (SPD) leaders. During the trial prosecutors read the *Manifesto* out loud as evidence; this meant that the pam-phlet could legally be published in Germany. Thus in 1872 Marx and Engels rushed out a new German-language edition, writing a preface that identified that several portions that became outdated in the quarter century since its orig-inal publication. This edition was also the first time the title was shortened to *The Communist Manifesto* (*Das Kommunistische Manifest*), and it became the bedrock the authors based future editions upon. Between 1871 and 1873, the *Manifesto* was published in over nine editions in six languages; in 1872 it was published in the United States for the first time, serialised in *Woodhull & Claflin's Weekly* of New York City. However, by the mid 1870s the *Communist Manifesto* remained Marx and Engels' only work to be even moderately well-known.

Over the next forty years, as social-democratic parties rose across Europe and parts of the world, so did the publication of the *Manifesto* alongside them, in hundreds of editions in thirty languages. Marx and Engels wrote a new preface for the 1882 Russian edition, translated by Georgi Plekhanov in Geneva. In it they wondered if Russia could directly become a communist society, or if she would become capitalist first like other European countries. After Marx's death in 1883, Engels alone provided the prefaces for five editions between 1888 and 1893. Among these is the 1888 English edition, translated by Samuel Moore and approved by Engels, who also provided notes throughout the text. It has been the standard English-language edition ever since.

The principal region of its influence, in terms of editions published, was in the "central belt of Europe", from Russia in the east to France in the west. In comparison, the pamphlet had little impact on politics in southwest and southeast Europe, and moderate presence in the north. Outside Europe, Chinese and Japanese translations were published, as were Spanish editions in Latin America. This uneven geographical spread in the *Manifesto*'s popularity reflected the development of socialist movements in a particular region as well as the popularity of Marxist variety of socialism there. There was not always a strong correlation between a social-democratic party's strength and the *Manifesto*'s popularity in that country. For instance, the German SPD printed only a few thousand copies of the *Communist Manifesto* every year, but a few hundred thousand copies of the *Erfurt Programme*. Further, the mass-based social-democratic parties of the Second International did not require their rank and file to be well-versed in theory; Marxist works such as the *Manifesto* or *Das Kapital* were read primarily by party theoreticians. On the other hand, small, dedicated militant parties and Marxist sects in the West took pride in knowing the theory; Hobsbawm says "This was the milieu in which 'the clearness of a comrade could be gauged invariably from the number of earmarks on his Manifesto'".

Figure 24: *The Bolshevik (1920) by Boris Kustodiev. Following the 1917 Bolshevik takeover of Russia Marx/Engels classics like the Communist Manifesto were distributed far and wide.*

Ubiquity, 1917–present

Following the October Revolution of 1917 that swept the Vladimir Lenin-led Bolsheviks to power in Russia, the world's first socialist state was founded explicitly along Marxist lines. The Soviet Union, which Bolshevik Russia would become a part of, was a one-party state under the rule of the Communist Party of the Soviet Union (CPSU). Unlike their mass-based counterparts of the Second International, the CPSU and other Leninist parties like it in the Third International expected their members to know the classic works of Marx, Engels and Lenin. Further, party leaders were expected to base their policy decisions on Marxist-Leninist ideology. Therefore works such as the *Manifesto* were required reading for the party rank-and-file.

Therefore the widespread dissemination of Marx and Engels' works became an important policy objective; backed by a sovereign state, the CPSU had relatively inexhaustible resources for this purpose. Works by Marx, Engels, and Lenin were published on a very large scale, and cheap editions of their works were available in several languages across the world. These publications were either shorter writings or they were compendia such as the various editions of Marx and Engels' *Selected Works*, or their *Collected Works*. This affected the destiny of the *Manifesto* in several ways. Firstly, in terms of circulation;

in 1932 the American and British Communist Parties printed several hundred thousand copies of a cheap edition for "probably the largest mass edition ever issued in English". Secondly the work entered political-science syllabuses in universities, which would only expand after the Second World War. For its centenary in 1948, its publication was no longer the exclusive domain of Marxists and academicians; general publishers too printed the *Manifesto* in large numbers. "In short, it was no longer only a classic Marxist document," Hobsbawm noted, "it had become a political classic *tout court.*"

Even after the collapse of the Soviet Bloc in the 1990s, the *Communist Manifesto* remains ubiquitous; Hobsbawm says that "In states without censorship, almost certainly anyone within reach of a good bookshop, and certainly anyone within reach of a good library, not to mention the internet, can have access to it." The 150th anniversary once again brought a deluge of attention in the press and the academia, as well as new editions of the book fronted by introductions to the text by academics. One of these, *The Communist Manifesto: A Modern Edition* by Verso, was touted by a critic in the *London Review of Books* as being a "stylish red-ribboned edition of the work. It is designed as a sweet keepsake, an exquisite collector's item. In Manhattan, a prominent Fifth Avenue store put copies of this choice new edition in the hands of shop-window mannequins, displayed in come-hither poses and fashionable décolletage."

Legacy

<templatestyles src="Template:Quote_box/styles.css" />

"With the clarity and brilliance of genius, this work outlines a new world-conception, consistent materialism, which also embraces the realm of social life; dialectics, as the most comprehensive and profound doctrine of development; the theory of the class struggle and of the world-historic revolutionary role of the proletariat—the creator of a new, communist society."

—Vladimir Lenin on the *Manifesto*, 1914[323]

A number of late-20th- and 21st-century writers have commented on the *Communist Manifesto*'s continuing relevance. In a special issue of the *Socialist Register* commemorating the *Manifesto*'s 150th anniversary, Peter Osborne argued that it was 'the single most influential text written in the nineteenth century.'[324] Academic John Raines in 2002 noted that "In our day this Capitalist Revolution has reached the farthest corners of the earth. The tool of money has produced the miracle of the new global market and the ubiquitous shopping mall. Read *The Communist Manifesto*, written more than one hundred and fifty years ago, and you will discover that Marx foresaw it all."[325] In 2003, the English Marxist Chris Harman stated, "There is still a compulsive quality to its prose as it provides insight after insight into the society in

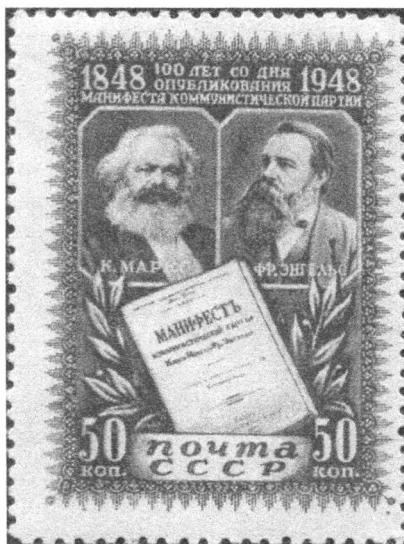

Figure 25: *Soviet Union stamp commemorating the 100th anniversary of the Manifesto*

which we live, where it comes from and where its going to. It is still able to explain, as mainstream economists and sociologists cannot, today's world of recurrent wars and repeated economic crisis, of hunger for hundreds of millions on the one hand and 'overproduction' on the other. There are passages that could have come from the most recent writings on globalisation."[326] Alex Callinicos, editor of *International Socialism*, stated in 2010 that "This is indeed a manifesto for the 21st century."[327] Writing in *The London Evening Standard* in 2012, Andrew Neather cited Verso Books' 2012 re-edition of *The Communist Manifesto*, with an introduction by Eric Hobsbawm, as part of a resurgence of left-wing-themed ideas which includes the publication of Owen Jones' best-selling *Chavs: The Demonization of the Working Class* and Jason Barker's documentary *Marx Reloaded*.

In contrast, critics such as Revisionist Marxist and reformist socialist Eduard Bernstein distinguished between "immature" early Marxism—as exemplified by the *Communist Manifesto* written by Marx and Engels in their youth—that he opposed for its violent Blanquist tendencies, and later "mature" Marxism that he supported.[328] This latter form refers to Marx in his later life acknowledging that socialism could be achieved through peaceful means through legislative reform in democratic societies.[329] Bernstein declared that the massive and homogeneous working-class claimed in the *Communist Manifesto* did not exist, and that contrary to claims of a proletarian majority emerging, the middle-class was growing under capitalism and not disappearing as Marx had claimed. Bernstein noted that the working-class was not homogeneous but heterogeneous, with divisions and factions within it, including socialist and non-socialist trade unions. Marx himself, later in his life, acknowledged that the middle-class was not disappearing in his work *Theories of Surplus Value* (1863). The obscurity of the later work means that Marx's acknowledgement of this error is not well known.[330] George Boyer described the *Manifesto* as "very much a period piece, a document of what was called the 'hungry' 1840s."

Many have drawn attention to the passage in the *Manifesto* that seems to sneer at the stupidity of the rustic: "The bourgeoisie ... draws all nations ... into civilisation ... It has created enormous cities ... and thus rescued a considerable part of the population from the idiocy [sic!] of rural life".[331] As Eric Hobsbawm noted, however:

<templatestyles src="Template:Quote/styles.css"/>

> *[W]hile there is no doubt that Marx at this time shared the usual towns-*
> *man's contempt for, as well as ignorance of, the peasant milieu, the ac-*
> *tual and analytically more interesting German phrase ("dem Idiotismus*
> *des Landlebens entrissen") referred not to "stupidity" but to "the narrow*
> *horizons", or "the isolation from the wider society" in which people in the*
> *countryside lived. It echoed the original meaning of the Greek term idiotes*
> *from which the current meaning of "idiot" or "idiocy" is derived, namely*
> *"a person concerned only with his own private affairs and not with those*
> *of the wider community". In the course of the decades since the 1840s,*
> *and in movements whose members, unlike Marx, were not classically ed-*
> *ucated, the original sense was lost and was misread.*

Influences

Marx and Engel's political influences were wide-ranging, reacting to and taking inspiration from German idealist philosophy, French socialism, and English and Scottish political economy. *The Communist Manifesto* also takes influence from literature. In Jacques Derrida's work, *Specters of Marx: The State of the Debt, the Work of Mourning and the New International*, he uses Shakespeare's *Hamlet* to frame a discussion of the history of the International, showing, in the process, the influence that Shakespeare's work had on Marx and Engel's writing.[332] In his essay, "Big Leagues: Specters of Milton and Republican International Justice between Shakespeare and Marx," Christopher N. Warren makes the case that English poet John Milton also had a substantial influence on Marx and Engel's work.[333] Historians of 19th-century reading habits have confirmed that Marx and Engels would have read these authors, and it is known that Marx loved Shakespeare, in particular.[334,335,336] Milton, Warren argues, also shows a notable influence on *The Communist Manifesto*: "Looking back on Milton's era, Marx saw a historical dialectic founded on inspiration in which freedom of the press, republicanism, and revolution were closely joined."[337] Milton's republicanism, Warren continues, served as "a useful, if unlikely, bridge" as Marx and Engels sought to forge a revolutionary international coalition.

References

<templatestyles src="Template:Refbegin/styles.css" />

- Adoratsky, V. (1938). *The History of the Communist Manifesto of Marx and Engels*. New York: International Publishers.
- Boyer, George R. (1998). "The Historical Background of the Communist Manifesto". *Journal of Economic Perspectives*. **12** (4): 151–74. CiteSeerX 10.1.1.673.9426[338] 𝖺 . doi: 10.1257/jep.12.4.151[339]. JSTOR 2646899[340].
- Hobsbawm, Eric (2011). "On the *Communist Manifesto*". *How To Change The World*. Little, Brown. pp. 101–20. ISBN 978-1-408-70287-1.
- Hunt, Tristram (2009). *Marx's General: The Revolutionary Life of Friedrich Engels*. Metropolitan Books.
- Schumpeter, Joseph (1997) [1952]. *Ten Great Economists: From Marx to Keynes*. London: Routledge. ISBN 978-0-415-11079-2.
- Schumpeter, Joseph A. (June 1949). "The *Communist Manifesto* in sociology and economics". *Journal of Political Economy*. The University of Chicago Press via JSTOR. **57** (3): 199–212. doi: 10.1086/256806[341]. JSTOR 1826126[342].

Source text

- Karl Marx, Friedrich Engels (2004) [1848]. *Manifesto of the Communist Party*[343]. Marxists Internet Archive. Retrieved on 14 March 2015.

External links

Wikisourcehas original text related to this article:
Manifesto of the Communist Party

Wikimedia Commons has media related to *Communist Manifesto*.

- *The Communist Manifesto*[344] at the Marxists Internet Archive
- *The Communist Manifesto*[345] in 80 world languages
- *Manifest der Kommunistischen Partei : veröffentlicht im Februar 1848*[346] Original 1848 edition in full color scan
- ◀) *The Communist Manifesto*[347] public domain audiobook at LibriVox
- *The Communist Manifesto*[348], a musical piece composed by Erwin Schulhoff, at YouTube
- On the *Communist Manifesto*[349] at modkraft.dk (a collection of links to bibliographical and historical materials, and contemporary analyses)

Marxian economics

Marxian economics

Part of a series on
Marxian economics

- **Economics portal**
- **Marxism portal**

- $\underline{v}$
- $\underline{t}$
- $\underline{e}^{350}$

Part of a series on

Marxism

-   Socialism portal
-   Communism portal
-   Philosophy portal

- v
- t
- e[351]

Marxian economics, or the **Marxian school of economics,** refers to a school of economic thought tracing its foundations to the critique of classical political economy first expounded upon by Karl Marx and Friedrich Engels. Marxian economics refers to several different theories and includes multiple schools of thought which are sometimes opposed to each other, and in many cases Marxian analysis is used to complement or supplement other economic approaches. Because one does not necessarily have to be politically Marxist to be economically Marxian, the two adjectives coexist in usage rather than being synonymous. They share a semantic field while also allowing connotative and denotative differences.

Marxian economics concerns itself variously with the analysis of crisis in capitalism, the role and distribution of the surplus product and surplus value in various types of economic systems, the nature and origin of economic value, the impact of class and class struggle on economic and political processes, and the process of economic evolution.

Marxian economics, particularly in academia, is distinguished from Marxism as a political ideology as well as the normative aspects of Marxist thought, with the view that Marx's original approach to understanding economics and economic development is intellectually independent from Marx's own advocacy of revolutionary socialism. Marxian economists do not lean entirely upon the works of Marx and other widely known Marxists, but draw from a range of Marxist and non-Marxist sources.[352]

Although the Marxian school is considered heterodox, ideas that have come out of Marxian economics have contributed to mainstream understanding of the global economy; certain concepts of Marxian economics, especially those related to capital accumulation and the business cycle, such as creative destruction, have been fitted for use in capitalist systems.Wikipedia:Citation needed

Marx's magnum opus on political economy was *Das Kapital* (*Capital: A Critique of Political Economy*) in three volumes, of which only the first volume was published in his lifetime (1867); the others were published by Friedrich Engels from Marx's notes. One of Marx's early works, *Critique of Political Economy*, was mostly incorporated into *Das Kapital*, especially the beginning of volume 1. Marx's notes made in preparation for writing *Das Kapital* were published in 1939 under the title *Grundrisse*.

Marx's response to classical economics

Marx's economics took as its starting point the work of the best-known economists of his day, the British classical economists Adam Smith, Thomas Robert Malthus and David Ricardo.

In *The Wealth of Nations* (1776), Smith argued that the most important characteristic of a market economy was that it permitted a rapid growth in productive abilities. Smith claimed that a growing market stimulated a greater "division of labor" (i.e. specialization of businesses and/or workers) and in turn this led to greater productivity. Although Smith generally said little about laborers, he did note that an increased division of labor could at some point cause harm to those whose jobs became narrower and narrower as the division of labor expanded. Smith maintained that a *laissez-faire* economy would naturally correct itself over time.

Marx followed Smith by claiming that the most important beneficial economic consequence of capitalism was a rapid growth in productivity abilities. Marx also expanded greatly on the notion that laborers could come to harm as capitalism became more productive. Additionally, Marx noted in *Theories of Surplus Value*: "We see the great advance made by Adam Smith beyond the Physiocrats in the analysis of surplus-value and hence of capital. In their view, it is only one definite kind of concrete labour—agricultural labour—that creates surplus-value.. But to Adam Smith, it is general social labour — no matter in what use-values it manifests itself — the mere quantity of necessary labour, which creates value. Surplus-value, whether it takes the form of profit, rent, or the secondary form of interest, is nothing but a part of this labour, appropriated by the owners of the material conditions of labour in the exchange with living labour".

Malthus' claim in *An Essay on the Principle of Population* (1798) that population growth was the primary cause of subsistence level wages for laborers provoked Marx to develop an alternative theory of wage determination. Whereas Malthus presented an ahistorical theory of population growth, Marx offered a theory of how a relative surplus population in capitalism tended to push wages to subsistence levels. Marx saw this relative surplus population as coming from economic causes and not from biological causes (as in Malthus). This economic-based theory of surplus population is often labeled as Marx's theory of the reserve army of labour.

Ricardo developed a theory of distribution within capitalism—that is, a theory of how the output of society is distributed to classes within society. The most mature version of this theory, presented in *On the Principles of Political Economy and Taxation* (1817), was based on a labour theory of value in which the value of any produced object is equal to the labor embodied in the object and Smith too presented a labor theory of value, but it was only incompletely realized. Also notable in Ricardo's economic theory was that profit was a deduction from society's output and that wages and profit were inversely related: an increase in profit came at the expense of a reduction in wages. Marx built much of the formal economic analysis found in *Capital* on Ricardo's theory of the economy.

Marx's theory

Marx employed a labour theory of value, which holds that the value of a commodity is the socially necessary labour time invested in it. In this model, capitalists do not pay workers the full value of the commodities they produce; rather, they compensate the worker for the necessary labor only (the worker's wage, which cover only the necessary means of subsistence in order to maintain him working in the present and his family in the future as a group). This necessary labor is necessarily only a fraction of a full working day - the rest, surplus-labor, would be pocketed by the capitalist as profit.

Marx theorized that the gap between the value a worker produces and his wage is a form of unpaid labour, known as surplus value. Moreover, Marx argues that markets tend to obscure the social relationships and processes of production; he called this commodity fetishism. People are highly aware of commodities, and usually don't think about the relationships and labor they represent.

Marx's analysis leads to the consideration of economic crisis. "A propensity to crisis—what we would call *business cycles*—was not recognised as an inherent feature of capitalism by any other economist of Marx's time," observed Robert Heilbroner in *The Worldly Philosophers*, "although future events have certainly indicated his prediction of successive boom and crash." Marx's theory of economic cycles was formalised by Richard Goodwin in "A Growth Cycle" (1967), a paper published during the centenary year of *Capital, Volume I*.

Methodology

Marx used dialectics, a method that he adapted from the works of Georg Wilhelm Friedrich Hegel. Dialectics focuses on relation and change, and tries to avoid seeing the universe as composed of separate objects, each with essentially stable unchanging characteristics. One component of dialectics is abstraction; out of an undifferentiated mass of data or system conceived of as an organic whole, one abstracts portions to think about or to refer to. One may abstract objects, but also—and more typically—relations, and processes of change. An abstraction may be extensive or narrow, may focus on generalities or specifics, and may be made from various points of view. For example, a sale may be abstracted from a buyer's or a seller's point of view, and one may abstract a particular sale or sales in general. Another component is the dialectical deduction of categories. Marx uses Hegel's notion of *categories*, which are *forms*, for economics: The commodity *form*, the money *form*, the capital *form* etc. have to be systematically deduced instead of being grasped in an outward way as done by the bourgeois economists. This corresponds to Hegel's critique of Kant's transcendental philosophy.[353]

Marx regarded history as having passed through several stages. The details of his periodisation vary somewhat through his works, but it essentially is: Primitive Communism – Slave societies – Feudalism – Capitalism – Socialism – Communism (capitalism being the present stage and communism the future). Marx occupied himself primarily with describing capitalism. Historians place the beginning of capitalism some time between about 1450 (Sombart) and some time in the 17th century (Hobsbawm).[354]

Marx defines a commodity as a product of human labour that is produced for sale in a market, and many products of human labour are commodities. Marx began his major work on economics, *Capital*, with a discussion of commodities; Chapter One is called "Commodities".

Commodities

"The wealth of those societies in which the capitalist mode of production prevails, presents itself as 'an immense accumulation of commodities,' its unit being a single commodity." (First sentence of *Capital,* Volume I.)

"The common substance that manifests itself in the exchange value of commodities whenever they are exchanged, is their value." (Capital, I, Chap I, section 1.)

The worth of a commodity can be conceived of in two different ways, which Marx calls use-value and value. A commodity's use-value is its usefulness for fulfilling some practical purpose; for example, the use-value of a piece of food is that it provides nourishment and pleasurable taste; the use value of a hammer, that it can drive nails.

Value is, on the other hand, a measure of a commodity's worth in comparison to other commodities. It is closely related to exchange-value, the ratio at which commodities should be traded for one another, but not identical: value is at a more general level of abstraction; exchange-value is a realisation or form of it.

Marx argued that if value is a property common to all commodities, then whatever it is derived from, whatever determines it, must be common to all commodities. The only relevant thing that is, in Marx's view, common to all commodities is human labour: they are all produced by human labour.

Marx concluded that the value of a commodity is simply the amount of human labour required to produce it. Thus Marx adopted a labour theory of value, as had his predecessors Ricardo and MacCulloch; Marx himself traced the existence of the theory at least as far back as an anonymous work, *Some Thoughts on the Interest of Money in General, and Particularly the Publick Funds, &c.,* published in London around 1739 or 1740.[355]

Marx placed some restrictions on the validity of his value theory: he said that in order for it to hold, the commodity must not be a useless item; and it is not the actual amount of labour that went into producing a particular individual commodity that determines its value, but the amount of labour that a worker of average energy and ability, working with average intensity, using the prevailing techniques of the day, would need to produce it. A formal statement of the law is: the value of a commodity is equal to the average socially necessary labour time required for its production. (Capital, I, Chap I – p. 39 in Progress Publishers, Moscow, ed'n.)

Marx's contention was that commodities tend, at a fairly general level of abstraction, to exchange at value; that is, if Commodity A, whose value is "V", is traded for Commodity B, it will tend to fetch an amount of Commodity B whose value is the same, "V". Particular circumstances will cause divergence from this rule, however.

Money

Marx held that metallic money, such as gold, is a commodity, and its value is the labour time necessary to produce it (mine it, smelt it, etc.). Marx argued that gold and silver are conventionally used as money because they embody a large amount of labour in a small, durable, form, which is convenient. Paper money is, in this model, a representation of gold or silver, almost without value of its own but held in circulation by state decree.

"Paper money is a token representing gold or money." (Capital, I, Chap III, section 2, part c)

Production

Marx lists the elementary factors of production as:

1. labour, "the personal activity of man." (Capital, I, VII, 1.)
2. the subject of labour: the thing worked on.
3. the instruments of labour: tools, labouring domestic animals like horses, chemicals used in modifying the subject, etc.

Some subjects of labour are available directly from Nature: uncaught fish, un-mined coal, etc. Others are results of a previous stage of production; these are known as raw materials, such as flour or yarn. Workshops, canals, and roads are considered instruments of labour. (*Capital*, I, VII, 1.) Coal for boilers, oil for wheels, and hay for draft horses is considered raw material, not instruments of labour.

"If, on the other hand, the subject of labour has, so to say, been filtered through previous labour, we call it raw material. . . ." (*Capital*, I, Chap VII, section 1.)

The subjects of labour and instruments of labour together are called the means of production. Relations of production are the relations human beings adopt toward each other as part of the production process. In capitalism, wage labour and private property are part of the relations of production.

Calculation of value of a product (price not to be confused with value):

If labour is performed directly on Nature and with instruments of negligible value, the value of the product is simply the labour time. If labour is performed on something that is itself the product of previous labour (that is, on a raw material), using instruments that have some value, the value of the product is the value of the raw material, plus depreciation on the instruments, plus the labour time. Depreciation may be figured simply by dividing the value of the instruments by their working life; *e.g.* if a lathe worth £1,000 lasts in use 10 years it imparts value to the product at a rate of £100 per year.

$value = mp + lt$,	Where:	$value$	is the value of the product;
		mp	is the value of the means of production;
		lt	is the labour time.

Effect of technical progress

According to Marx, the amount of actual product (i.e. use-value) that a typical worker produces in a given amount of time is the productivity of labour. It has tended to increase under capitalism. This is due to increase in the scale of enterprise, to specialisation of labour, and to the introduction of machinery. The immediate result of this is that the value of a given item tends to decrease, because the labour time necessary to produce it becomes less.

In a given amount of time, labour produces more items, but each unit has less value; the total value created per time remains the same. This means that the means of subsistence become cheaper; therefore the value of labour power or necessary labour time becomes less. If the length of the working day remains the same, this results in an increase in the surplus labour time and the rate of surplus value.

Technological advancement tends to increase the amount of capital needed to start a business, and it tends to result in an increasing preponderance of capital being spent on means of production (constant capital) as opposed to labour (variable capital). Marx called the ratio of these two kinds of capital the composition of capital.

Current theorizing in Marxian economics

Marxian economics has been built upon by many others, beginning almost at the moment of Marx's death. The second and third volumes of *Das Kapital* were edited by his close associate Friedrich Engels, based on Marx's notes. Marx's *Theories of Surplus Value* was edited by Karl Kautsky. The Marxian value theory and the Perron-Frobenius theorem on the positive eigenvector of a positive matrix are fundamental to mathematical treatments of Marxist economics.

The Universities offering one or more courses in Marxian economics, or teach one or more economics courses on other topics from a perspective that they designate as Marxian or Marxist, include Colorado State University, New School for Social Research, School of Oriental and African Studies, Universiteit Maastricht, University of Bremen, University of California, Riverside,

University of Leeds, University of Maine, University of Manchester, University of Massachusetts Amherst, University of Massachusetts Boston, University of Missouri–Kansas City, University of Sheffield, University of Utah, and York University (Toronto).[356]

English-language journals include *Capital & Class*, *Historical Materialism*, *Monthly Review*, *Rethinking Marxism*, *Review of Radical Political Economics*, and *Studies in Political Economy*.

Criticisms

Much of the critique of classical Marxian economics came from Marxian economists that revised Marx's original theory, or by the Austrian school of economics. V. K. Dmitriev, writing in 1898,[357] Ladislaus von Bortkiewicz, writing in 1906–07,[358] and subsequent critics claimed that Marx's value theory and law of the tendency of the rate of profit to fall are internally inconsistent. In other words, the critics allege that Marx drew conclusions that actually do not follow from his theoretical premises. Once these alleged errors are corrected, his conclusion that aggregate price and profit are determined by, and equal to, aggregate value and surplus value no longer holds true. This result calls into question his theory that the exploitation of workers is the sole source of profit.[359]

Whether the rate of profit in capitalism has, as Marx predicted, tended to fall is a subject of debate. N. Okishio, in 1961, devised a theorem (Okishio's theorem) showing that if capitalists pursue cost-cutting techniques and if the real wage does not rise, the rate of profit must rise.[360]

The inconsistency allegations have been a prominent feature of Marxian economics and the debate surrounding it since the 1970s.[361]

Among the critics pointing out internal inconsistencies are former and current Marxian and/or Sraffian economists, such as Paul Sweezy,[362] Nobuo Okishio,[363] Ian Steedman,[364] John Roemer,[365] Gary Mongiovi, and David Laibman,[366] who propose that the field be grounded in their correct versions of Marxian economics instead of in Marx's critique of political economy in the original form in which he presented and developed it in *Capital*.[367]

Proponents of the Temporal Single System Interpretation (TSSI) of Marx's value theory claim that the supposed inconsistencies are actually the result of misinterpretation; they argue that when Marx's theory is understood as "temporal" and "single-system," the alleged internal inconsistencies disappear. In a recent survey of the debate, a proponent of the TSSI concludes that "the *proofs* of inconsistency are no longer defended; the entire case against Marx has been reduced to the *interpretive* issue."[368]

Relevance to economics

Marxist economics was assessed as lacking relevance in 1988 by Robert M. Solow, who criticized the New Palgrave Dictionary of Economics for oversampling articles on Marxism themes, giving a "false impression of the state of play" in the economics profession. Solow stated that "Marx was an important and influential thinker, and Marxism has been a doctrine with intellectual and practical influence. The fact is, however, that most serious English-speaking economists regard Marxist economics as an irrelevant dead end."[369]

"Economists working in the Marxian-Sraffian tradition represent a small minority of modern economists, and that their writings have virtually no impact upon the professional work of most economists in major English-language universities", according to George Stigler.

Neo-Marxian economics

The terms *Neo-Marxian*, *Post-Marxian*, and *Radical Political Economics* were first used to refer to a distinct tradition of economic thought in the 1970s and 1980s.

In industrial economics, the Neo-Marxian approach stresses the monopolistic rather than the competitive nature of capitalism. This approach is associated with Michal Kalecki, Paul A. Baran and Paul Sweezy.[370,371]

References

<templatestyles src="Template:Refbegin/styles.css" />

- Glyn, Andrew (1987). "Marxist economics". *The New Palgrave: A Dictionary of Economics*. **3**. pp. 390–95. doi: 10.1057/978-1-349-95121-5_1135-1[372].
- Roemer, J. E. (1987). "Marxian value analysis". *The New Palgrave: A Dictionary of Economics*. **3**. pp. 383–87. doi: 10.1057/978-1-349-95121-5_1001-1[373].
- John E. Roemer (2008). "socialism (new perspectives)," *The New Palgrave Dictionary of Economics*, 2nd Edition, Abstract.[374]
- Diane Flaherty (2008). "radical economics," *The New Palgrave Dictionary of Economics*, 2nd Edition, Abstract.[375]
- Lenny Flank, 'Contradictions of Capitalism: An Introduction to Marxist Economics', St Petersburg, Florida: Red and Black Publishers, 2007. ISBN 978-0-9791813-9-9.
- Heilbroner, Robert (2000). *The Worldly Philosophers* (7th ed.). London: Penguin Books. ISBN 978-0-140-29006-6.

- Screpanti, Ernesto; Zamagni, Stefano (2005). *An Outline of the History of Economic Thought* (2nd ed.). Oxford: Oxford University Press. ISBN 978-0-199-27913-5.
- Thomas T. Sexine, *The Dialectic of Capital. A Study of the Inner Logic of Capitalism*, 2 volumes (preliminary edition), Tokyo 1986; OCLC 489902822[376] (vol. 1), OCLC 873921143[377] (vol. 2).
- Solow, Robert M. (20 March 1988). "The Wide, Wide World Of Wealth (*The New Palgrave: A Dictionary of Economics'*. Edited by John Eatwell, Murray Milgate and Peter Newman. Four volumes. 4,103 pp. New York: Stockton Press. $650)"[378]. *New York Times.*

Further reading

- Althusser, Louis and Balibar, Étienne. *Reading Capital.* London: Verso, 2009.
- Bottomore, Tom, ed. *A Dictionary of Marxist Thought.* Oxford: Blackwell, 1998.
- Cochrane, James L. (1970). "Marxian Macroeconomics". *Macroeconomics Before Keynes.* Glenview: Scott, Foresman & Co. pp. 43–58. OCLC 799965716[379].
- Fine, Ben. *Marx's Capital.* 5th ed. London: Pluto, 2010.
- Harvey, David. *A Companion to Marx's Capital.* London: Verso, 2010.
- Harvey, David. *The Limits of Capital.* London: Verso, 2006.
- Mandel, Ernest. *Marxist Economic Theory.* New York: Monthly Review Press, 1970.
- Mandel, Ernest. *The Formation of the Economic Thought of Karl Marx.* New York: Monthly Review Press, 1977.
- Morishima, Michio. *Marx's Economics: A Dual Theory of Value and Growth.* Cambridge: Cambridge University Press, 1973.
- Postone, Moishe. *Time, Labor, and Social Domination: A Reinterpretation of Marx's Critical Theory.* Cambridge [England]: Cambridge University Press, 1993.
- Saad-Filho, Alfredo. *The Value of Marx: Political Economy for Contemporary Capitalism.* London: Routledge, 2002.
- Wolff, Richard D. and Resnick, Stephen A. *Contending Economic Theories: Neoclassical, Keynesian, and Marxian.* The MIT Press, 2012. ISBN 0262517833

External links

- Marxian Economics[380] (archive[381] from Schwartz center of economic policy analysis[382])
- Marxian Political Economy[383]
- The Neo-Marxian Schools[384] (archive[385] from Schwartz center of economic policy analysis[382])
- A Marxian Introduction to Modern Economics[386]
- International working group on value theory[387]
- An outline of Marxist economics[388], Chapter 6 of *Reformism or Revolution* by Alan Woods
- The End of the Market[389] A website containing a critical evaluation the idea of the market-clearing price which affirms Marx's theory that in capitalism profitability would decline
- The Neo-Marxian Schools ("Radical Political Economy")[390]
- *If you're so smart, why aren't you rich?*[391] Monthly Review article detailing the degeneration of Marxian economics.

Marxism

Marxism

Marxism is a method of socioeconomic analysis that views class relations and social conflict using a materialist interpretation of historical development and takes a dialectical view of social transformation. It originates from the works of 19th century German philosophers Karl Marx and Friedrich Engels.

Marxism uses a methodology, now known as historical materialism, to analyze and critique the development of capitalism and the role of class struggles in systemic economic change.

According to Marxist theory, class conflict arises in capitalist societies due to contradictions between the material interests of the oppressed proletariat—a class of wage labourers employed by the bourgeoisie to produce goods and services—and the bourgeoisie—the ruling class that owns the means of production and extract their wealth through appropriation of the surplus product (profit) produced by the proletariat.

This class struggle that is commonly expressed as the revolt of a society's productive forces against its relations of production, results in a period of short-term crises as the bourgeoisie struggle to manage the intensifying alienation of labor experienced by the proletariat, albeit with varying degrees of class consciousness. This crisis culminates in a proletarian revolution and eventually leads to the establishment of socialism—a socioeconomic system based on social ownership of the means of production, distribution based on one's contribution and production organized directly for use. As the productive forces continued to advance, Marx hypothesized that socialism would ultimately transform into a communist society; a classless, stateless, humane society based on common ownership and the underlying principle: "From each according to his ability, to each according to his needs".

Marxism has developed into many different branches and schools of thought, though now there is no single definitive Marxist theory. Different Marxian schools place a greater emphasis on certain aspects of classical Marxism while rejecting or modifying other aspects. Many schools of thought have sought to combine Marxian concepts and non-Marxian concepts, which has then led to contradictory conclusions. However, lately there is movement toward the recognition that historical materialism and dialectical materialism remains the fundamental aspect of all Marxist schools of thought, which should result in more agreement between different schools.

Marxism has had a profound and influential impact on global academia and has expanded into many fields such as archaeology, anthropology,[393] media studies,[394] political science, theater, history, sociology, art history and theory, cultural studies, education, economics, ethics, criminology, geography, literary criticism, aesthetics, film theory, critical psychology and philosophy.[395]

Figure 26: *Karl Marx (1818–1883)*

Etymology

The term "Marxism" was popularized by Karl Kautsky, who considered himself an "orthodox" Marxist during the dispute between the orthodox and revisionist followers of Marx.[396] Kautsky's revisionist rival Eduard Bernstein also later adopted use of the term. Engels did not support the use of the term "Marxism' to describe either Marx's or his views.[397] Engels claimed that the term was being abusively used as a rhetorical qualifier by those attempting to cast themselves as "real" followers of Marx while casting others in different terms, such as "Lassallians". In 1882, Engels claimed that Marx had criticized self-proclaimed "Marxist" Paul Lafargue, by saying that if Lafargue's views were considered "Marxist", then "one thing is certain and that is that I am not a Marxist".

Overview

Marxism analyzes the material conditions and the economic activities required to fulfill human material needs to explain social phenomena within any given society.

It assumes that the form of economic organization, or mode of production, influences all other social phenomena—including social relations, political institutions, legal systems, cultural systems, aesthetics, and ideologies. The economic system and these social relations form a base and superstructure.

As forces of production, i.e. technology, improve, existing forms of social organization become obsolete and hinder further progress. As Karl Marx observed: "At a certain stage of development, the material productive forces of society come into conflict with the existing relations of production or—this merely expresses the same thing in legal terms—with the property relations within the framework of which they have operated hitherto. From forms of development of the productive forces these relations turn into their fetters. Then begins an era of social revolution".[398] These inefficiencies manifest themselves as social contradictions in society in the form of class struggle.[399]

Under the capitalist mode of production, this struggle materializes between the minority (the bourgeoisie) who own the means of production and the vast majority of the population (the proletariat) who produce goods and services. Starting with the conjectural premise that social change occurs because of the struggle between different classes within society who are under contradiction against each other, a Marxist would conclude that capitalism exploits and oppresses the proletariat, therefore capitalism will inevitably lead to a proletarian revolution.

Marxian economics and its proponents view capitalism as economically unsustainable and incapable of improving the living standards of the population due to its need to compensate for falling rates of profit by cutting employee's wages, social benefits and pursuing military aggression. The socialist system would succeed capitalism as humanity's mode of production through workers' revolution. According to Marxian crisis theory, socialism is not an inevitability, but an economic necessity.[400]

In a socialist society, private property—in the form of the means of production—would be replaced by co-operative ownership. A socialist economy would not base production on the creation of private profits, but on the criteria of satisfying human needs—that is, production would be carried out directly for use. As Friedrich Engels said: "Then the capitalist mode of appropriation in which the product enslaves first the producer, and then appropriator, is replaced by the mode of appropriation of the product that is based upon the nature of the modern means of production; upon the one hand, direct social appropriation, as means to the maintenance and extension of production on the other, direct individual appropriation, as means of subsistence and of enjoyment".[401]

Historical materialism

<templatestyles src="Template:Quote_box/styles.css" />

The discovery of the materialist conception of history, or rather, the consistent continuation and extension of materialism into the domain of social phenomenon, removed two chief defects of earlier historical theories. In the first place, they at best examined only the ideological motives of the historical activity of human beings, without grasping the objective laws governing the development of the system of social relations ... in the second place, the earlier theories did not cover the activities of the *masses* of the population, whereas historical materialism made it possible for the first time to study with the accuracy of the natural sciences the social conditions of the life of the masses and the changes in these conditions.

— Russian Marxist theoretician and revolutionary Vladimir Lenin, 1913[402]

<templatestyles src="Template:Quote/styles.css"/>

> *Society does not consist of individuals, but expresses the sum of interrelations, the relations within which these individuals stand.*
>
> *—Karl Marx, Grundrisse, 1858*[403]

The materialist theory of history[404] analyses the underlying causes of societal development and change from the perspective of the collective ways that humans make their living. All constituent features of a society (social classes, political pyramid, ideologies) are assumed to stem from economic activity, an idea often portrayed with the metaphor of the base and superstructure.

The base and superstructure metaphor describes the totality of social relations by which humans produce and re-produce their social existence. According to Marx: "The sum total of the forces of production accessible to men determines the condition of society" and forms a society's economic base. The base includes the material forces of production, that is the labour and material means of production and relations of production, i.e., the social and political arrangements that regulate production and distribution. From this base rises a superstructure of legal and political "forms of social consciousness" of political and legal institutions that derive from the economic base that conditions the superstructure and a society's dominant ideology. Conflicts between the development of material productive forces and the relations of production provokes social revolutions and thus the resultant changes to the economic base will lead to the transformation of the superstructure.[405] This relationship is reflexive, as at first the base gives rise to the superstructure and remains the foundation of a form of social organization, hence that formed social organization can act again upon both parts of the base and superstructure so that the relationship is not static but a dialectic, expressed and driven by conflicts and contradictions. As Engels clarified: "The history of all hitherto existing society is the history of class struggles. Freeman and slave, patrician and ple- beian, lord and serf, guild-master and journeyman, in a word, oppressor and oppressed, stood in constant opposition to one another, carried on uninter- rupted, now hidden, now open fight, a fight that each time ended, either in a revolutionary reconstitution of society at large, or in the common ruin of the contending classes".[406]

Marx considered class conflicts as the driving force of human history since these recurring conflicts have manifested themselves as distinct transitional stages of development in Western Europe. Accordingly, Marx designated hu- man history as encompassing four stages of development in relations of pro- duction:[407]

1. Primitive communism: as in co-operative tribal societies.
2. Slave society: a development of tribal to city-state; aristocracy is born.
3. Feudalism: aristocrats are the ruling class; merchants evolve into capital- ists.
4. Capitalism: capitalists are the ruling class, who create and employ the proletariat.

Criticism of capitalism

According to the Marxist theoretician and revolutionary Vladimir Lenin, "the principal content of Marxism" was "Marx's economic doctrine".[408] Marx be- lieved that the capitalist bourgeois and their economists were promoting what he saw as the lie that "the interests of the capitalist and of the worker are ... one and the same", therefore he believed that they did this by purporting the concept that "the fastest possible growth of productive capital" was best not only for the wealthy capitalists but also for the workers because it provided them with employment.[409]

Exploitation is a matter of surplus labour—the amount of labour one performs beyond what one receives in goods. Exploitation has been a socioeconomic feature of every class society and is one of the principal features distinguish- ing the social classes. The power of one social class to control the means of production enables its exploitation of the other classes.

In capitalism, the labour theory of value is the operative concern; the value of a commodity equals the socially necessary labour time required to produce it. Under that condition, surplus value (the difference between the value produced and the value received by a labourer) is synonymous with the term "surplus labour", thus capitalist exploitation is realised as deriving surplus value from the worker.

· In pre-capitalist economies, exploitation of the worker was achieved via physical coercion. In the capitalist mode of production, that result is more subtly achieved and because workers do not own the means of production, they must voluntarily enter into an exploitive work relationship with a capitalist in order to earn the necessities of life. The worker's entry into such employment is voluntary in that they choose which capitalist to work for. However, the worker must work or starve, thus exploitation is inevitable and the "voluntary" nature of a worker participating in a capitalist society is illusory.

Alienation is the estrangement of people from their humanity (German: *Gattungswesen*, "species-essence", "species-being"), which is a systematic result of capitalism. Under capitalism, the fruits of production belong to the employers, who expropriate the surplus created by others and so generate alienated labourers.[410] In Marx's view, alienation is an objective characterization of the worker's situation in capitalism—his or her self-awareness of this condition is not prerequisite.

Social classes

Marx distinguishes social classes on the basis of two criteria: ownership of means of production and control over the labour power of others. Following this criterion of class based on property relations, Marx identified the social stratification of the capitalist mode of production with the following social groups:

- Proletariat: "[...] the class of modern wage labourers who, having no means of production of their own, are reduced to selling their labour power in order to live." The capitalist mode of production establishes the conditions enabling the bourgeoisie to exploit the proletariat because the workers' labour generates a surplus value greater than the workers' wages.
- Bourgeoisie: those who "own the means of production" and buy labour power from the proletariat, thus exploiting the proletariat. They subdivide as bourgeoisie and the petite bourgeoisie.
  - Petite bourgeoisie are those who work and can afford to buy little labour power i.e. small business owners, peasant landlords, trade workers and the like. Marxism predicts that the continual reinvention of the means of production eventually would destroy the petite bourgeoisie, degrading them from the middle class to the proletariat.
- Lumpenproletariat: the outcasts of society such as the criminals, vagabonds, beggars, or prostitutes without any political or class consciousness. Having no interest in international or national economics affairs, Marx claimed that this specific sub-division of the proletariat would play no part in the eventual social revolution.

- Landlords: a historically important social class who retain some wealth and power.
- Peasantry and farmers: a scattered class incapable of organizing and effecting socio-economic change, most of whom would enter the proletariat while some would become landlords.

Class consciousness denotes the awareness—of itself and the social world—that a social class possesses and its capacity to rationally act in their best interests, hence class consciousness is required before they can effect a successful revolution and thus the dictatorship of the proletariat.

Without defining ideology,[411] Marx used the term to describe the production of images of social reality. According to Engels, "ideology is a process accomplished by the so-called thinker consciously, it is true, but with a false consciousness. The real motive forces impelling him remain unknown to him; otherwise it simply would not be an ideological process. Hence he imagines false or seeming motive forces".[412] Because the ruling class controls the society's means of production, the superstructure of society (the ruling social ideas), are determined by the best interests of the ruling class. In *The German Ideology*, he says "[t]he ideas of the ruling class are in every epoch the ruling ideas, i.e., the class which is the ruling material force of society, is, at the same time, its ruling intellectual force."

The term "political economy" initially referred to the study of the material conditions of economic production in the capitalist system. In Marxism, political economy is the study of the means of production, specifically of capital and how that manifests as economic activity.

<templatestyles src="Template:Quote_box/styles.css" />

Marxism taught me what society was. I was like a blindfolded man in a forest, who doesn't even know where north or south is. If you don't eventually come to truly understand the history of the class struggle, or at least have a clear idea that society is divided between the rich and the poor, and that some people subjugate and exploit other people, you're lost in a forest, not knowing anything.

— Cuban revolutionary and Marxist–Leninist politician Fidel Castro on discovering Marxism, 2009[413]

This new way of thinking was invented because socialists believed that common ownership of the "means of production" (that is the industries, the land, the wealth of nature, the trade apparatus, the wealth of the society, etc.) will abolish the exploitative working conditions experienced under capitalism. Through working class revolution, the state (which Marxists see as a weapon for the subjugation of one class by another) is seized and used to suppress the hitherto ruling class of capitalists and by implementing a commonly-owned, democratically controlled workplace create the society of communism, which Marxists see as true democracy. An economy based on co-operation on human need and social betterment, rather than competition for profit of many independently acting profit seekers, would also be the end of class society, which Marx saw as the fundamental division of all hitherto existing history.

Marx saw work, the effort by humans to transform the environment for their needs, as a fundamental feature of human kind. Capitalism, in which the product of the worker's labor is taken from them and sold at market rather than being part of the worker's life, is therefore alienating to the worker. Additionally, the worker is compelled by various means (some nicer than others) to work harder, faster and for longer hours. While this is happening, the employer is constantly trying to save on labor costs: pay the workers less, figure out how to use cheaper equipment, etc. This allows the employer to extract the largest mount of work (and therefore potential wealth) from their workers. The fundamental nature of capitalist society is no different from that of slave society: one small group of society exploiting the larger group.

Through common ownership of the means of production, the profit motive is eliminated and the motive of furthering human flourishing is introduced. Because the surplus produced by the workers is property of the society as whole, there are no classes of producers and appropriators. Additionally, the state, which has its origins in the bands of retainers hired by the first ruling classes to protect their economic privilege, will disappear as its conditions of existence have disappeared.[414]

Revolution, socialism and communism

According to orthodox Marxist theory, the overthrow of capitalism by a socialist revolution in contemporary society is inevitable. While the inevitability of an eventual socialist revolution is a controversial debate among many different Marxist schools of thought, all Marxists believe socialism is a necessity, if not inevitable. Marxists believe that a socialist society is far better for the majority of the populace than its capitalist counterpart. Prior to the Russian revolution of 1917, Lenin wrote: "The socialization of production is bound to lead to the conversion of the means of production into the property of society ... This conversion will directly result in an immense increase in productivity of labour, a reduction of working hours, and the replacement of the remnants, the ruins of small-scale, primitive, disunited production by collective and improved labour".[415] The failure of the 1905 revolution and the failure of socialist movements to resist the outbreak of World War One led to renewed theoretical effort and valuable contributions from Lenin and

Figure 27: *Leftist protester wielding a red flag with a raised fist, both are symbols of revolutionary socialism.*

Rosa Luxemburg towards an appreciation of Marx's crisis theory and efforts to formulate a theory of imperialism.[416]

Classical Marxism

"Classical Marxism" denotes the collection of socio-eco-political theories expounded by Karl Marx and Friedrich Engels. "Marxism", as Ernest Mandel remarked, "is always open, always critical, always self-critical". As such, classical Marxism distinguishes between "Marxism" as broadly perceived and "what Marx believed", thus in 1883 Marx wrote to the French labour leader Jules Guesde and to Marx's son-in-law Paul Lafargue—both of whom claimed to represent Marxist principles—accusing them of "revolutionary phrase-mongering" and of denying the value of reformist struggle.

From Marx's letter derives the paraphrase:

"If that is Marxism, then I am not a Marxist".[417]

American Marxist scholar Hal Draper responded to this comment by saying:

"There are few thinkers in modern history whose thought has been so badly misrepresented, by Marxists and anti-Marxists alike".[418]

On the other hand, the book *Communism: The Great Misunderstanding* argues that the source of such misrepresentations lies in ignoring the philosophy of Marxism, which is dialectical materialism. In large, this was due to the fact that *The German Ideology*, in which Marx and Engels developed this philosophy, did not find a publisher for almost one hundred years.

Figure 28: *One of the 20th century's most prominent Marxist academics, the Australian archaeologist V. Gordon Childe*

Academic Marxism

Marxism has been adopted by a large number of academics and other scholars working in various disciplines.

The theoretical development of Marxist archaeology was first developed in the Soviet Union in 1929, when a young archaeologist named Vladislav I. Ravdonikas (1894–1976) published a report entitled "For a Soviet history of material culture" Within this work, the very discipline of archaeology as it then stood was criticised as being inherently bourgeois, therefore anti-socialist and so, as a part of the academic reforms instituted in the Soviet Union under the administration of Premier Joseph Stalin, a great emphasis was placed on the adoption of Marxist archaeology throughout the country.[419] These theoretical developments were subsequently adopted by archaeologists working in capitalist states outside of the Leninist bloc, most notably by the Australian academic V. Gordon Childe (1892–1957), who used Marxist theory in his understandings of the development of human society.[420]

Marxist sociology is the study of sociology from a Marxist perspective.[421] Marxist sociology is "a form of conflict theory associated with ... Marxism's objective of developing a positive (empirical) science of capitalist society as part of the mobilization of a revolutionary working class".[422] The American

Sociological Association has a section dedicated to the issues of Marxist sociology that is "interested in examining how insights from Marxist methodology and Marxist analysis can help explain the complex dynamics of modern society".[423] Influenced by the thought of Karl Marx, Marxist sociology emerged during the end of the 19th and beginning of the 20th century. As well as Marx, Max Weber and Émile Durkheim are considered seminal influences in early sociology. The first Marxist school of sociology was known as Austro-Marxism, of which Carl Grünberg and Antonio Labriola were among its most notable members. During the 1940s, the Western Marxist school became accepted within Western academia, subsequently fracturing into several different perspectives such as the Frankfurt School or critical theory. Due to its former state-supported position, there has been a backlash against Marxist thought in post-communist states (see sociology in Poland) but it remains dominant in the sociological research sanctioned and supported by those communist states that remain (see sociology in China).

Marxian economics refers to a school of economic thought tracing its foundations to the critique of classical political economy first expounded upon by Karl Marx and Friedrich Engels. Marxian economics concerns itself with the analysis of crisis in capitalism, the role and distribution of the surplus product and surplus value in various types of economic systems, the nature and origin of economic value, the impact of class and class struggle on economic and political processes, and the process of economic evolution. Although the Marxian school is considered heterodox, ideas that have come out of Marxian economics have contributed to mainstream understanding of the global economy. Certain concepts of Marxian economics, especially those related to capital accumulation and the business cycle, such as creative destruction, have been fitted for use in capitalist systems.

Marxist historiography is a school of historiography influenced by Marxism. The chief tenets of Marxist historiography are the centrality of social class and economic constraints in determining historical outcomes. Marxist historiography has made contributions to the history of the working class, oppressed nationalities, and the methodology of history from below. Friedrich Engels' most important historical contribution was *Der deutsche Bauernkrieg* (*The German Peasants' War*), which analysed social warfare in early Protestant Germany in terms of emerging capitalist classes. *The German Peasants' War* indicate the Marxist interest in history from below and class analysis, and attempts a dialectical analysis. Engels' short treatise *The Condition of the Working Class in England in 1844* (1870s) was salient in creating the socialist impetus in British politics. Marx's most important works on social and political history include *The Eighteenth Brumaire of Louis Napoleon*, *The Communist Manifesto*, *The German Ideology*, and those chapters of *Das Kapital* dealing with the historical emergence of capitalists and proletarians from pre-industrial English society. Marxist historiography suffered in the Soviet Union, as the government requested overdetermined historical writing. Notable histories include the *Short Course History of the Communist Party of the Soviet Union (Bolshevik)*, published in the 1930s to justify the nature of Bolshevik party life under Joseph Stalin. A circle of historians inside the Communist Party of Great Britain (CPGB) formed in 1946. While some members of the group (most notably Christopher Hill and E. P. Thompson) left the CPGB after the 1956 Hungarian Revolution, the common points of British Marxist historiography continued in their works. Thompson's *The Making of the English Working Class* is one of the works commonly associated with this group. Eric Hobsbawm's *Bandits* is another example of this group's work. C. L. R. James was also a great pioneer of the 'history from below' approach. Living in Britain when he wrote his most notable work *The Black Jacobins* (1938), he was an anti-Stalinist Marxist and so outside of the CPGB. In India, B. N. Datta and D. D. Kosambi are considered the founding fathers of Marxist historiography. Today, the seniormost scholars of Marxist historiography are R. S. Sharma, Irfan Habib, Romila Thapar, D. N. Jha and K. N. Panikkar, most of whom are now over 75 years old.[424]

Marxist literary criticism is a loose term describing literary criticism based on socialist and dialectic theories. Marxist criticism views literary works as reflections of the social institutions from which they originate. According to Marxists, even literature itself is a social institution and has a specific ideological function, based on the background and ideology of the author. Notable marxist literary critics include Mikhail Bakhtin, Walter Benjamin, Terry Eagleton and Fredric Jameson. Marxist aesthetics is a theory of aesthetics based on, or derived from, the theories of Karl Marx. It involves a dialectical and materialist, or dialectical materialist, approach to the application of Marxism to the cultural sphere, specifically areas related to taste such as art, beauty, etc. Marxists believe that economic and social conditions, and especially the class relations that derive from them, affect every aspect of an individual's life, from religious beliefs to legal systems to cultural frameworks. Some notable Marxist aestheticians include Anatoly Lunacharsky, Mikhail Lifshitz, William Morris, Theodor W. Adorno, Bertolt Brecht, Herbert Marcuse, Walter Benjamin, Antonio Gramsci, Georg Lukács, Louis Althusser, Jacques Rancière, Maurice Merleau-Ponty and Raymond Williams.

According to a 2007 survey of American professors by Neil Gross and Solon Simmons, 17.6% of social science professors and 5.0% of humanities professors identify as Marxists, while between 0 and 2% of professors in all other disciplines identify as Marxists.

Figure 29: *Friedrich Engels*

History

Karl Marx and Friedrich Engels

Karl Marx (5 May 1818 – 14 March 1883) was a German philosopher, political economist and socialist revolutionary who addressed the matters of alienation and exploitation of the working class, the capitalist mode of production and historical materialism. He is famous for analysing history in terms of class struggle, summarised in the initial line introducing *The Communist Manifesto* (1848): "The history of all hitherto existing society is the history of class struggles".[425]

Friedrich Engels (28 November 1820 – 5 August 1895) was a German political philosopher who together with Marx co-developed communist theory. Marx and Engels first met in September 1844. Discovering that they had similar views of philosophy and socialism, they collaborated and wrote works such as *Die heilige Familie* (*The Holy Family*). After Marx was deported from France in January 1845, they moved to Belgium, which then permitted greater freedom of expression than other European countries. In January 1846, they returned to Brussels to establish the Communist Correspondence Committee.

In 1847, they began writing *The Communist Manifesto* (1848), based on Engels' *The Principles of Communism*. Six weeks later, they published

Figure 30: *Fidel Castro at the UN General Assembly, 1960*

the 12,000-word pamphlet in February 1848. In March, Belgium expelled them and they moved to Cologne, where they published the *Neue Rheinische Zeitung*, a politically radical newspaper. By 1849, they had to leave Cologne for London. The Prussian authorities pressured the British government to expel Marx and Engels, but Prime Minister Lord John Russell refused.

After Marx's death in 1883, Engels became the editor and translator of Marx's writings. With his *Origins of the Family, Private Property, and the State* (1884) – analysing monogamous marriage as guaranteeing male social domination of women, a concept analogous, in communist theory, to the capitalist class's economic domination of the working class—Engels made intellectually significant contributions to feminist theory and Marxist feminism.

Late 20th century

In 1959, the Cuban Revolution led to the victory of Fidel Castro and his July 26 Movement. Although the revolution was not explicitly socialist, upon victory Castro ascended to the position of Prime Minister and adopted the Leninist model of socialist development, forging an alliance with the Soviet Union.[426] One of the leaders of the revolution, the Argentine Marxist revolutionary Che Guevara (1928–1967), subsequently went on to aid revolutionary socialist movements in Congo-Kinshasa and Bolivia, eventually being killed by the Bolivian government, possibly on the orders of the Central Intelligence Agency (CIA), though the CIA agent sent to search for Guevara, Felix Rodriguez, expressed a desire to keep him alive as a possible bargaining tool with the Cuban government. He would posthumously go on to become an internationally recognised icon.

In the People's Republic of China, the Maoist government undertook the Cultural Revolution from 1966 through to 1976 to ameliorate capitalist elements of Chinese society and achieve socialism. However, upon Mao Zedong's death, his rivals seized political power and under the Premiership of Deng Xiaoping (1978–1992), many of Mao's Cultural Revolution era policies were revised or abandoned and much of the state sector privatised.

The late 1980s and early 1990s saw the collapse of most of those socialist states that had professed a Marxist–Leninist ideology. In the late 1970s and early 1980s, the emergence of the New Right and neoliberal capitalism as the dominant ideological trends in western politics—championed by U.S. President Ronald Reagan and U.K. Prime Minister Margaret Thatcher—led the west to take a more aggressive stand against the Soviet Union and its Leninist allies. Meanwhile, in the Soviet Union the reformist Mikhael Gorbachev became Premier in March 1985 and sought to abandon Leninist models of development towards social democracy. Ultimately, Gorbachev's reforms, coupled with rising levels of popular ethnic nationalism in the Soviet Union, led to the state's dissolution in late 1991 into a series of constituent nations, all of which abandoned Marxist–Leninist models for socialism, with most converting to capitalist economies.

21st century

At the turn of the 21st century, China, Cuba, Laos, North Korea and Vietnam remained the only officially Marxist–Leninist states remaining, although a Maoist government led by Prachanda was elected into power in Nepal in 2008 following a long guerrilla struggle.

The early 21st century also saw the election of socialist governments in several Latin American nations, in what has come to be known as the "pink tide". Dominated by the Venezuelan government of Hugo Chávez, this trend also saw the election of Evo Morales in Bolivia, Rafael Correa in Ecuador and Daniel Ortega in Nicaragua. Forging political and economic alliances through international organisations like the Bolivarian Alliance for the Americas, these socialist governments allied themselves with Marxist–Leninist Cuba and although none of them espoused a Leninist path directly, most admitted to being significantly influenced by Marxist theory.

Figure 31: *Hugo Chavez casting a vote in 2007*

Figure 32: *Xi Jinping in 2016*

For Italian Marxist Gianni Vattimo in his 2011 book *Hermeneutic Communism*, "this new weak communism differs substantially from its previous Soviet (and current Chinese) realization, because the South American countries follow democratic electoral procedures and also manage to decentralize the state bureaucratic system through the Bolivarian missions. In sum, if weakened communism is felt as a specter in the West, it is not only because of media distortions but also for the alternative it represents through the same democratic procedures that the West constantly professes to cherish but is hesitant to apply".[427]

Chinese President Xi Jinping has announced a deepening commitment of the Chinese Communist Party to the ideas of Marx. At an event celebrating the 200th anniversary of Marx's birth, Xi said "We must win the advantages, win the initiative, and win the future. We must continuously improve the ability to use Marxism to analyse and solve practical problems..." also adding "powerful ideological weapon for us to understand the world, grasp the law, seek the truth, and change the world,". Xi has further stressed the importance of examining and continuing the tradition of the CPC and embrace its revolutionary past.

Criticism

Criticisms of Marxism have come from various political ideologies and academic disciplines. These include general criticisms about lack of internal consistency, criticisms related to historical materialism, that it is a type of historical determinism, the necessity of suppression of individual rights, issues with the implementation of communism and economic issues such as the distortion or absence of price signals and reduced incentives. In addition, empirical and epistemological problems are frequently identified.[428,429]

Some Marxists have criticised the academic institutionalisation of Marxism for being too shallow and detached from political action. For instance, Zimbabwean Trotskyist Alex Callinicos, himself a professional academic, stated: "Its practitioners remind one of Narcissus, who in the Greek legend fell in love with his own reflection ... Sometimes it is necessary to devote time to clarifying and developing the concepts that we use, but indeed for Western Marxists this has become an end in itself. The result is a body of writings incomprehensible to all but a tiny minority of highly qualified scholars".[430]

Additionally, there are intellectual critiques of Marxism that contest certain assumptions prevalent in Marx's thought and Marxism after him, without exactly rejecting Marxist politics.[431] Other contemporary supporters of Marxism argue that many aspects of Marxist thought are viable, but that the corpus is incomplete or outdated in regards to certain aspects of economic, political or social theory. They may therefore combine some Marxist concepts with the ideas of other theorists such as Max Weber—the Frankfurt School is one example.[432]

General criticisms

Philosopher and historian of ideas Leszek Kołakowski pointed out that "Marx's theory is incomplete or ambiguous in many places, and could be 'applied' in many contradictory ways without manifestly infringing its principles". Specifically, he considers "the laws of dialectics" as fundamentally erroneous, stating that some are "truisms with no specific Marxist content", others "philosophical dogmas that cannot be proved by scientific means" and some just "nonsense". He believes that some Marxist laws can be interpreted differently, but that these interpretations still in general fall into one of the two categories of error.

Okishio's theorem shows that if capitalists use cost-cutting techniques and real wages do not increase, the rate of profit must rise, which casts doubt on Marx's view that the rate of profit would tend to fall.[433]

The allegations of inconsistency have been a large part of Marxian economics and the debates around it since the 1970s.[434] Andrew Kliman argues that this undermines Marx's critiques and the correction of the alleged inconsistencies, because internally inconsistent theories cannot be right by definition.[435]

Epistemological and empirical critiques

Marx's predictions have been criticized because they have allegedly failed, with some pointing towards the GDP per capita increasing generally in capitalist economies compared to less market oriented economics, the capitalist economies not suffering worsening economic crises leading to the overthrow of the capitalist system and communist revolutions not occurring in the most advanced capitalist nations, but instead in undeveloped regions.[436]

In his books *The Poverty of Historicism* and *Conjectures and Refutations*, philosopher of science Karl Popper, criticized the explanatory power and validity of historical materialism. Popper believed that Marxism had been initially scientific, in that Marx had postulated a genuinely predictive theory. When these predictions were not in fact borne out, Popper argues that the theory avoided falsification by the addition of ad hoc hypotheses that made it compatible with the facts. Because of this, Popper asserted, a theory that was initially genuinely scientific degenerated into pseudoscientific dogma.

Socialist critiques

Democratic socialists and social democrats reject the idea that socialism can be accomplished only through extra-legal class conflict and a proletarian revolution. The relationship between Marx and other socialist thinkers and organizations—rooted in Marxism's "scientific" and anti-utopian socialism, among other factors—has divided Marxists from other socialists since Marx's life.

After Marx's death and with the emergence of Marxism, there have also been dissensions within Marxism itself—a notable example is the splitting of the Russian Social Democratic Labour Party into Bolsheviks and Mensheviks. Orthodox Marxists became opposed to a less dogmatic, more innovative, or even revisionist Marxism.

Anarchist and libertarian critiques

Anarchism has had a strained relationship with Marxism since Marx's life. Anarchists and many non-Marxist libertarian socialists reject the need for a transitory state phase, claiming that socialism can only be established through decentralized, non-coercive organization. Anarchist Mikhail Bakunin criticized Marx for his authoritarian bent. The phrases "barracks socialism" or "barracks communism" became a shorthand for this critique, evoking the image of citizens' lives being as regimented as the lives of conscripts in a barracks. Noam Chomsky is critical of Marxism's dogmatic strains and the idea of Marxism itself, but still appreciates Marx's contributions to political thought. Unlike some anarchists, Chomsky does not consider Bolshevism "Marxism in practice", but he does recognize that Marx was a complicated figure who had conflicting ideas, while he also acknowledges the latent authoritarianism in Marx he also points to the libertarian strains that developed into the council communism of Rosa Luxemburg and Anton Pannekoek. However, his commitment to libertarian socialism has led him to characterize himself as an anarchist with radical Marxist leanings (see political positions of Noam Chomsky).

Libertarian Marxism refers to a broad scope of economic and political philosophies that emphasize the anti-authoritarian aspects of Marxism. Early currents of libertarian Marxism, known as left communism, emerged in opposition to Marxism–Leninism[437] and its derivatives such as Stalinism, Ceaușism and Maoism. Libertarian Marxism is also often critical of reformist positions, such as those held by social democrats. Libertarian Marxist currents often draw from Marx and Engels' later works, specifically the *Grundrisse* and *The Civil War in France*,[438] emphasizing the Marxist belief in the ability of the working class to forge its own destiny without the need for a revolutionary party or state to mediate or aid its liberation.[439] Along with anarchism, libertarian Marxism is one of the main currents of libertarian socialism.[440]

Economic critiques

Other critiques come from an economic standpoint. Vladimir Karpovich Dmitriev writing in 1898,[441] Ladislaus von Bortkiewicz writing in 1906–1907[442] and subsequent critics have alleged that Marx's value theory and law of the tendency of the rate of profit to fall are internally inconsistent. In other words, the critics allege that Marx drew conclusions that actually do not follow from his theoretical premises. Once these alleged errors are corrected, his conclusion that aggregate price and profit are determined by and equal to aggregate value and surplus value no longer holds true. This result calls into question his theory that the exploitation of workers is the sole source of profit.[443]

Both Marxism and socialism have received considerable critical analysis from multiple generations of Austrian economists in terms of scientific methodology, economic theory and political implications.[444,445] During the marginal revolution, subjective value theory was rediscovered by Carl Menger, a development that fundamentally undermined the British cost theories of value. The restoration of subjectivism and praxeological methodology previously used by classical economists including Richard Cantillon, Anne-Robert-Jacques Turgot, Jean-Baptiste Say and Frédéric Bastiat led Menger to criticise historicist methodology in general. Second-generation Austrian economist Eugen Böhm von Bawerk used praxeological and subjectivist methodology to attack the law of value fundamentally. Non-Marxist economists have regarded his criticism as definitive, with Gottfried Haberler arguing that Böhm-Bawerk's critique of Marx's economics was so thorough and devastating that as of the 1960s no Marxian scholar had conclusively refuted it.[446] Third-generation Austrian Ludwig von Mises rekindled debate about the economic calculation problem by identifying that without price signals in capital goods, all other aspects of the market economy are irrational. This led him to declare that "rational economic activity is impossible in a socialist commonwealth".

Daron Acemoglu and James A. Robinson argue that Marx's economic theory was fundamentally flawed because it attempted to simplify the economy into a few general laws that ignored the impact of institutions on the economy.

References

Bibliography

<templatestyles src="Template:Refbegin/styles.css" />

- Bourne, Peter (1986). *Fidel: A Biography of Fidel Castro*. New York: Dodd, Mead & Company.
- Callinicos, Alex (2010) [1983]. *The Revolutionary Ideas of Karl Marx*. Bloomsbury, London: Bookmarks. ISBN 978-1-905192-68-7.
- Castro, Fidel; Ramonet, Ignacio (interviewer) (2009). *My Life: A Spoken Autobiography*. New York: Scribner. ISBN 978-1-4165-6233-7.
- Coltman, Leycester (2003). *The Real Fidel Castro*. New Haven and London: Yale University Press. ISBN 978-0-300-10760-9.
- Green, Sally (1981). *Prehistorian: A Biography of V. Gordon Childe*. Bradford-on-Avon, Wiltshire: Moonraker Press. ISBN 978-0-239-00206-8.
- Lenin, Vladimir (1967) [1913]. *Karl Marx: A Brief Biographical Sketch with an Exposition of Marxism*[447]. Peking: Foreign Languages Press. Retrieved 17 June 2014.
- Marx, Karl (1849). *Wage Labour and Capital*[448]. Germany: Neue Rheinische Zeitung. Retrieved 2014-06-17.
- Trigger, Bruce G. (2007). *A History of Archaeological Thought* (2nd ed.). New York: Cambridge University Press. ISBN 978-0-521-60049-1.

- Agar, Jolyon (2006), *Rethinking Marxism: From Kant and Hegel to Marx and Engels* (London and New York: Routledge) ISBN 041541119X
- Avineri, Shlomo (1968). *The Social and Political Thought of Karl Marx*. Cambridge University Press.
- Dahrendorf, Ralf (1959). *Class and Class Conflict in Industrial Society*. Stanford, CA: Stanford University Press.
- Jon Elster, *An Introduction to Karl Marx*. Cambridge, England, 1986.
- Michael Evans, *Karl Marx*. London, 1975.
- Kołakowski, Leszek (1976). *Main Currents of Marxism*. Oxford University Press.
- Parkes, Henry Bamford (1939). *Marxism: An Autopsy*. Boston: Houghton Mifflin.
- Robinson, Cedric J.: *Black Marxism: The Making of the Black Radical Tradition*, 1983, Reissue: Univ North Carolina Press, 2000
- Rummel, R.J. (1977) *Conflict In Perspective*[449] Chap. 5 *Marxism, Class Conflict, and the Conflict Helix*[450]
- Screpanti, E; S. Zamagna (1993). *An Outline of the History of Economic Thought*.
- McLellan, David (2007). *Marxism After Marx*. Basingstoke: Palgrave Macmillan.

External links

Library resources about
Marxism

- Resources in your library[451]
- Resources in other libraries[452]

Wikimedia Commons has media related to *Marxism*.

Appendix

References

[1] Marx became a Fellow http://www.calmview2.eu/RSA/CalmViewA/Record.aspx?src= CalmView.Catalog&id=RSA%2fSC%2fIM%2f701%2fS1000&pos=9 of the highly prestigious Royal Society of Arts, London, in 1862.

[2] http://willamette.edu/cla/classics/careers/marx/index.html

[3] Bhikhu Parekh, *Marx's Theory of Ideology*, Routledge, 2015, p. 203.

[4] The name "Karl Heinrich Marx", used in various lexicons, is based on an error. His birth certificate says "Carl Heinrich Marx", and elsewhere "Karl Marx" is used. "K. H. Marx" is used only in his poetry collections and the transcript of his dissertation; because Marx wanted to honour his father, who had died in 1838, he called himself "Karl Heinrich" in three documents. The article https://archive.org/stream/handwrterbuchder04conr#page/1130/mode/1up by Friedrich Engels "Marx, Karl Heinrich" in *Handwörterbuch der Staatswissenschaften* (Jena, 1892, column 1130 to 1133 see *MECW* Volume 22, pp. 337–345) does not justify assigning Marx a middle name. See Heinz Monz: *Karl Marx. Grundlagen zu Leben und Werk*. NCO-Verlag, Trier 1973, p. 214 and 354, respectively.

[5] Karl Marx: *Critique of the Gotha Program* http://www.marxists.org/archive/marx/works/1875/gotha/index.htm

[6] Roberto Mangabeira Unger. *Free Trade Reimagined: The World Division of Labor and the Method of Economics*. Princeton: Princeton University Press, 2007.

[7] John Hicks, "Capital Controversies: Ancient and Modern." *The American Economic Review* 64.2 (May 1974) p 307: "The greatest economists, Smith or Marx or Keynes, have changed the course of history ..."

[8] Joseph Schumpeter Ten Great Economists: From Marx to Keynes. Volume 26 of Unwin University books. Edition 4, Taylor & Francis Group, 1952 , 9780415110785

[9] ; ; .

[10] ; ; .

[11] ; .

[12] Raddatz *Karl Marx: A Political Biography*

[13] Wheen 2001. pp. 12–13.

[14] ; ; .

[15] ; ; .

[16] *Francis Wheen, Karl Marx: A Life*, (Fourth Estate, 1999),

[17] ; .

[18] ; ; .

[19] ; ; .

[20] ; .

[21] ; .

[22] ; ; .

[23] ; ; .

[24] ; ; ; .

[25] ; ; .

[26] ; .

[27] ; .

[28] ; ; .

[29] ; ; .

[30] ; .

[31] ; . These love poems would be published posthumously in the *Collected Works of Karl Marx and Frederick Engels: Volume 1* (New York: International Publishers, 1975) pp. 531–632.

[32] ; .

[33] Marx's thesis was posthumously published in the *Collected Works of Karl Marx and Frederick Engels: Volume 1* (New York: International Publishers, 1975) pp. 25–107.

[34] Wheen 2001. p. 32.

[35] ; , .

[36] http://willamette.edu/cla/classics/careers/marx/index.html

[37] ; , .

[38] , .

[39] ; , .

[40] ; , .

[41] ; , .

[42] ; .

[43] ; , .

[44] ; , .

[45] Marx, Karl, "Contribution to the Critique of Hegel's Philosophy of Law", contained in the *Collected Works of Karl Marx and Frederick Engels: Volume 3* (International Publishers: New York, 1975) p. 3.

[46] Marx, Karl, "On the Jewish Question", contained in the *Collected Works of Karl Marx and Frederick Engels: Volume 3*, p. 146.

[47] ; , .

[48] , .

[49] Wheen 2001. p. 75.

[50] Mansel, Philip: *Paris Between Empires*, p. 390 (St. Martin Press, NY) 2001

[51] Frederick Engels, "The Condition of the Working Class in England", contained in the *Collected Works of Karl Marx and Frederick Engels: Volume 4* (International Publishers: New York, 1975) pp. 295–596.

[52] P. N. Fedoseyev, *Karl Marx: A Biography* (Progress Publishers: Moscow, 1973) p. 82.

[53] Wheen 2001. pp. 85–86.

[54] Karl Marx, "The Holy Family", contained in the *Collected Works of Karl Marx and Frederick Engels: Volume 4*, pp. 3–211.

[55] Taken from the caption of a picture of the house in a group of pictures located between pages 160 and 161 in the book "Karl Marx: A Biography", written by a team of historians and writers headed by P. N. Fedoseyev (Progress Publishers: Moscow, 1973).

[56] P. N. Fedoseyev, *et al. Karl Marx: A Biography*, p. 63.

[57] Isaiah Berlin, *Karl Marx: His Life and Environment* (Oxford University Press: London, 1963) pp. 90–94.

[58] P. N. Fedoseyev *et al.*, *Karl Marx: A Biography* (Progress Publishers: Moscow, 1973) p. 62.

[59] Larisa Miskievich, "Preface" to Volume 28 of the *Collected Works of Karl Marx and Frederick Engels* (International Publishers: New York, 1986) p. XII

[60] Karl Marx, *Collected Works of Karl Marx and Frederick Engels: Volume 35, Volume 36* and *Volume 37* (International Publishers: New York, 1996, 1997 and 1987).

[61] Isaiah Berlin, *Karl Marx: His Life and Environment*, pp. 35–61.

[62] P. N. Fedoseyev, *et al.*, *Karl Marx: A Biography*, p. 62.

[63] Note 54 contained on page 598 in the *Collected Works of Karl Marx and Frederick Engels: Volume 3*.

[64] Karl Marx, "Economic and Philosophical Manuscripts of 1844" *Collected Works of Karl Marx and Frederick Engels: Volume 3* (International Publishers: New York, 1975) pp. 229–346.

[65] P. N. Fedoseyev, *Karl Marx: A Biography*, p. 83.

[66] Karl Marx, "Theses on Feuerbach", contained in the *Collected Works of Karl Marx and Frederick Engels: Volume 5* (International Publishers: New York, 1976) pp. 3–14.

[67] Karl Marx, "Theses on Feuerbach," contained in the *Collected Works of Karl Marx and Frederick Engels: Volume 5*, p. 8.

[68] Heinrich Gemkow *et al.*, *Frederick Engels: A Biography* (Verlag Zeit im Bild ["New Book Publishing House"]: Dresden, 1972) p. 101

[69] Heinrich Gemkow, *et al.*, *Frederick Engels: A Biography*, p. 102.

[70] Heinrich Gemkow, *et al.*, *Frederick Engels: A Biography* (Verlag Zeit im Bild [New Book Publishing House]: Dresden, 1972) p. 53

[71] Heinrich Gemkow, *et al.*, *Frederick Engels: A Biography*, p. 78.

[72] P. N. Fedoseyev, *et al.*, *Karl Marx: A Biography*, p. 89.

[73] Wheen 2001. p. 92.

[74] Karl Marx and Frederick Engels, "German Ideology" contained in the *Collected Works of Karl Marx and Frederick Engels: Volume 5* (International Publishers: New York, 1976) pp. 19–539.

[75] P. N. Fedoseyev, *et al.*, *Karl Marx: A Biography*, pp. 96–97.

[76] Wheen 2001. p. 93.

[77] See Note 71 on p. 672 of the *Collected Works of Karl Marx and Frederick Engels: Volume 6* (International Publishers: New York, 1976).

[78] Karl Marx, *The Poverty of Philosophy* contained in the *Collected Works of Karl Marx and Frederick Engels: Volume 6*(International Publishers: New York, 1976) pp. 105–212.

[79] Wheen 2001. p. 107.

[80] P. N. Fedoseyev, *Karl Marx: A Biography* (Progress Publishers, Moscow, 1973) p. 124.

[81] Note 260 contained in the *Collected Works of Karl Marx and Frederick Engels: Volume 11* (International Publishers: New York, 1979) pp. 671–672.

[82] Note 260 contained in the *Collected Works of Karl Marx and Frederick Engels: Volume 11*, p. 672.

[83] P. N. Fedoseyev,*et al.*, *Karl Marx: A Biography*, pp. 123–125.

[84] P. N. Fedoseyev, *et al*, *Karl Marx: A Biography*, p. 125.

[85] Frederick Engels, "Principles of Communism" contained in the *Collected Works of Karl Marx and Frederick Engels: Volume 6* (International Publishers, New York, 1976) pp. 341–357.

[86] Karl Marx and Frederick Engels, "The Communist Manifesto" contained in the *Collected Works of Karl Marx and Frederick Engels: Volume 6*, pp. 477–519.

[87] Wheen 2001. p. 115.

[88] Marx and Engels 1848.

[89] Saul Kussiel Padover, *Karl Marx, an intimate biography*, McGraw-Hill, 1978, page 205

[90] David McLellan 1973 *Karl Marx: His life and Thought*. New York: Harper and Row. pp. 189–190

[91] Wheen 2001. p. 128.

[92] Karl Marx and Frederick Engels, "Demands of the Communist Party" contained in the *Collected Works of Karl Marx and Frederick Engels: Volume 7* (International Publishers: New York, 1977) pp. 3–6.

[93] Wheen 2001. p. 129.

[94] Wheen 2001. pp. 130–132.

[95] Seigel, p. 50

[96] Wheen 2001. pp. 137–146.

[97] Wheen 2001. pp. 147–148.

[98] P. N. Fedoseyev, *Karl Marx: A Biography*, p. 233.

[99] Note 269 contained on page 674 in the *Collected Works of Karl Marx and Frederick Engels: Volume 11*.

[100] Wheen 2001. pp. 151–155.

[101] Note 269 on page 674 of the *Collected Works of Karl Marx and Frederick Engels: Volume 11*.

[102] Jonathan Sperber, *Karl Marx: A Nineteenth-Century Life*, p. 295.

[103] P. N. Fedoseyev, *Karl Marx: A Biography*, 274.

[104] Taken from a picture on page 327 of the *Collected Works of Karl Marx and Frederick Engels: Volume 11* (International Publishers: New York, 1979).

[105] Karl Marx, "The Elections in England – Tories and Whigs" contained in the*Collected Works of Karl Marx and Frederick Engels: Volume 11* (International Publishers: New York, 1979) pp. 327–332.

[106] Marx & Engels Collected Works, vol.41 https//ia801605.us.archive.org

[107] Richard Kluger, *The Paper: The Life and Death of the New York Herald Tribune* (Alfred A. Knopf Publishing, New York, 1986) p. 121.

[108] Note 1 at page 367 contained in the *Collected Works of Karl Marx and Frederick Engels: Volume 19* (International Publishers: New York, 1984).

[109] Karl Marx, "The Eighteenth Brumaire of Louis Napoleon" contained in the *Collected Works of KarlMarx and Frederick Engels: Volume 11* (International Publishers: New York, 1979) pp. 99–197.

[110] Jonathan Sperber, *Karl Marx: A Nineteenth-Century*, p. 320.

[111] Jonathan Sperber, *Karl Marx: A Nineteenth-Century Life*, p. 347.

[112] P. N. Fedoseyev *et al.*, *Karl Marx: A Biography*, p. 345.

[113] Karl Marx, "The Civil War in France" contained in the *Collected Works of Karl Marx and Frederick Engels: Volume 22* (International Publishers: New York, 1986) pp. 307–359.

[114] Karl Marx, "Economic Manuscripts of 1857–1858" contained in the *Collected Works of Karl Marx and Frederick Engels: Volume 28* (International Publishers: New York, 1986) pp. 5–537.

[115] Karl Marx, "Economic Manuscripts of 1857–1858" contained in the Preparatory Materials section of the *Collected Works of Karl Marx and Frederick Engels: Volume 29* (International Publishers: New York, 1987) pp. 421–507.

[116] Karl Marx, "A Contribution to the Critique of Political Economy" contained in the *Collected Works of Karl Marx and Frederick Engels: Volume 29*, pp. 257–417.

[117] P. N. Fedoseyev, *Karl Marx: A Biography*, p. 318.

[118] See footnote #2 on the bottom of page 360 in the *Collected Works of Karl Marx and Frederick Engels: Volume 35*.

[119] Thomas Hodgskin, *Labour Defended against the Claims of Capital* (London, 1825) p. 25.

[120] Karl Marx, "Capital II: The Process of Circulation of Capital" embodying the whole volume of the *Collected Works of Karl Marx and Frederick Engels: Volume 36* (International Publishers: New York, 1997).

[121] Karl Marx, "Capital III: The Process of Capitalist Production as a Whole" embodying the whole volume of the *Collected Works of Karl Marx and Frederick Engels: Volume 37* (International Publishers: New York, 1998).

[122] Karl Marx, "Theories of Surplus Value" contained in the *Collected Works of Karl Marx and Frederick Engels: Volume 30* (International Publishers: New York, 1988) pp. 318–451.

[123] Karl Marx, "Theories of Surplus Value" contained in the *Collected Works of Karl Marx and Frederick Engels: Volume 31* (International Publishers: New York, 1989) pp. 5–580.

[124] Karl Marx, "Theories of Surplus Value" contained in the *Collected Works of Karl Marx and Frederick Engels: Volume 32* (International Publishers: New York, 1989) pp. 5–543.

[125] See note 228 on page 475 of the *Collected Works of Karl Marx and Frederick Engels: Volume 30*.

[126] Karl Marx and Frederick Engels, *Collected Works Volume 46* (International Publishers: New York, 1992) p. 71.

[127] K. Marx, First draft of letter to Vera Zasulich [1881]. In Marx-Engels 'Collected Works', Volume 24, p. 346.

[128] Peter Singer (2000). *Marx a very short introduction*. p. 5.

[129] Blumenberg, 98.

[130] Blumenberg, 100.

[131] Blumenberg, 99–100.

[132] Blumenberg, 98; Siegel, 494.

[133] Seigel, 495-6.

[134] Shuster, 1–2.

[135] Shuster, 3.

[136] Wheen 2001. p. 382 https://books.google.com/books?id=3KOyuSakn80C&pg=PA382.

[137] "Tomb raiders' failed attack on Marx grave" http://www.camdennewjournal.co.uk/111705/cn111705_11.htm, *Camden New Journal*

[138] Hobsbawm 2011. pp. 03–04.

[139] //en.wikipedia.org/w/index.php?title=Template:Marxism&action=edit

[140] Plutarch, Biography of Lycurgus http://classics.mit.edu/Plutarch/lycurgus.html

[141] Eaglelton, Terry *Why Marx Was Right* Yale University Press, 2011, p. 158

[142] Seigel, Jerrold *Marx's Fate* Princeton University Press, 1978, pp. 112–19

[143] Annelien de Dijn, *French Political Thought from Montesquieu to Tocqueville* https://books.google.com/books?id=a3SFelqBLw8C&dq=, Cambridge University Press, 2008, p. 152.

[144] Karl Marx. *Capital: A Critique of Political Economy*, vol. 1, trans. Samuel Moore and Edward Aveling (New York: Modem Library, 1906), 440.

[145] Marx K (1999). "The labour-process and the process of producing surplus-value". http://www.marxists.org/archive/marx/works/1867-c1/ch07.htm In K Marx, *Capital* (Vol. 1, Ch. 7). Marxists.org. Retrieved 20 October 2010. Original work published 1867.

[146] See Marx K (1997). "Critique of Hegel's dialectic and philosophy in general". In K Marx, *Writings of the Young Marx on Philosophy and Society* (LD Easton & KH Guddat, Trans.), pp. 314–347. Indianapolis: Hackett Publishing Company, Inc. Original work published 1844.

[147] See also Lefever DM; Lefever JT (1977). "Marxian alienation and economic organisation: An alternate view". *The American Economist(21)*2, pp. 40–48.

[148] See also Holland EW (2005). "Desire". In CJ Stivale (Ed.), *Gilles Deleuze: Key Concepts*, pp. 53–62. Montreal & Kingston: McGill-Queens University Press.

[149] Marx (1997), p. 321, emphasis in original.

[150] Marx (1997), p. 324.

[151]

[152] Karl Marx: Introduction http://www.marxists.org/archive/marx/works/1843/critique-hpr/intro. htm to A Contribution to the Critique of Hegel's Philosophy of Right, in: *Deutsch-Französische Jahrbücher*, February 1844

[153] In *The Communist Manifesto*, Part II:Proletariats and Communist and *Capital, Volume I*, Part III

[154] "You know that the institutions, mores, and traditions of various countries must be taken into consideration, and we do not deny that there are countries – such as America, England, and if I were more familiar with your institutions, I would perhaps also add Holland – where the workers can attain their goal by peaceful means. This being the case, we must also recognise the fact that in most countries on the Continent the lever of our revolution must be force; it is force to which we must some day appeal to erect the rule of labour." La Liberté Speech http://www.marxists. org/archive/marx/works/1872/09/08.htm delivered by Karl Marx on 8 September 1872, in Amsterdam

[155] Kevin B. Anderson (2016). " *Marx at the Margins: On Nationalism, Ethnicity, and Non-Western Societies https://books.google.com/books?id=TxCZCwAAQBAJ&pg=PA239*". University of Chicago Press. pp.49-239.

[156] Cited in: B. Hepner, "Marx et la puissance russe," in: K. Marx, *La Russie et l'Europe*, Paris, 1954, p. 20. Originally published in *Neue Rheinische Zeitung*, no. 223, 16 February 1849.

[157] Karl Marx and Friedrich Engels to the Chairman of the Slavonic Meeting, 21 March 1881. Source: Karl Marx and Frederick Engels, *Selected Correspondence* (Progress Publishers, Moscow, 1975).

[158] Speech delivered in London, probably to a meeting of the International's General Council and the Polish Workers Society on 22 January 1867, text published in *Le Socialisme*, 15 March 1908; *Odbudowa Polski* (Warsaw, 1910), pp. 119–23; *Mysl Socjalistyczna*, May 1908. From Karl Marx and Frederick Engels, *The Russian Menace to Europe*, edited by Paul Blackstock and Bert Hoselitz, and published by George Allen and Unwin, London, 1953, pp. 104–08.

[159] " Karl Marx and the Irish https://www.nytimes.com/1971/12/01/archives/karl-marx-and-the-irish.html". *The New York Times*. December 1971.

[160] Wheen, Francis (17 July 2005). "Why Marx is man of the moment" http://observer.guardian. co.uk/comment/story/0,6903,1530250,00.html. *The Observer*.

[161] Ricoeur, Paul. *Freud and Philosophy: An Essay on Interpretation*. New Haven and London: Yale University Press. 1970, p. 32

[162] Löwith, Karl. *From Hegel to Nietzsche*. New York: Columbia University Press, 1991, p. 49.

[163] Berlin, Isaiah. 1967. *Karl Marx: His Life and Environment*. Time Inc Book Division, New York. pp130

[164] Bridget O'Laughlin (1975) *Marxist Approaches in Anthropology*, Annual Review of Anthropology Vol. 4: pp. 341–70 (October 1975) .
William Roseberry (1997) *Marx and Anthropology* Annual Review of Anthropology, Vol. 26: pp. 25–46 (October 1997)

[165] See Manuel Alvarado, Robin Gutch, and Tana Wollen (1987) *Learning the Media: Introduction to Media Teaching*, Palgrave Macmillan.

[166] Kołakowski, Leszek. Main Currents of Marxism : the Founders, the Golden Age, the Breakdown. Translated by P. S. Falla. New York: W.W. Norton & Company, 2005.

[167] Aron, Raymond. Main Currents in Sociological Thought. Garden City, N.Y: Anchor Books, 1965.

[168] Anderson, Perry. Considerations on Western Marxism. London: NLB, 1976.

[169] Hobsbawm, E. J. How to Change the World : Marx and Marxism, 1840–2011 (London: Little, Brown, 2011), 314–344.

[170] Hemingway, Andrew. *Marxism and the History of Art: From William Morris to the New Left*. Pluto Press, 2006.

[171] " Nehru's economic philosophy http://www.thehindu.com/opinion/op-ed/nehrus-economic-philosophy/article18589548.ece". *The Hindu*. 27 May 2017.

[172] " Nelson Mandela's Living Legacy | Preparing for Defiance 1949-1952 https://www.thesouthafrican.com/nelson-mandelas-living-legacy-embracing-communism-and-the-defiance-campaign-1949-1952/". *The South African*. 6 November 2013.

[173] " Juncker opens exhibition to Karl Marx http://www.euronews.com/2018/05/04/juncker-opens-exhibition-to-karl-marx". *Euronews*. 4 Mary 2018

[174]

[175] https://books.google.com/books?id=6mq-H3EcUx8C

[176] http://www.marxists.org/archive/vygodsky/1965/discovery.htm

[177] https://archive.org/details/MarxBiographyGDR

[178] //doi.org/10.1093/ref%3Aodnb/39021

[179] http://www.oxforddnb.com/help/subscribe#public

[180] http://www.marxists.org/archive/lenin/works/1914/granat/index.htm

[181] http://lea.vitis.uspnet.usp.br/arquivos/artkarlmarxanoverviewofhisbiographies.pdf

[182] http://pubs.socialistreviewindex.org.uk/isj85/morgan.htm

[183] https://web.archive.org/web/20150318044953/http://www.findarticles.com/p/articles/mi_m1134/is_7_108/ai_55698600/pg_1

[184] http://www.findarticles.com/

[185] //www.jstor.org/stable/202551

[186] //doi.org/10.1111/j.1365-2133.2007.08282.x

[187] //www.ncbi.nlm.nih.gov/pubmed/17986303

[188] https://www.gutenberg.org/author/Marx,+Karl

[189] https//archive.org

[190] https://librivox.org/author/2426

[191] http://www.zeno.org/Philosophie/M/Marx,%20Karl

[192] https://www.britannica.com/EBchecked/topic/367265

[193] https://plato.stanford.edu/entries/marx/

[194] http://www.marxists.org/archive/marx/

[195] https://archive.org/details/KarlMarxABiography

[196] http://www.marxists.org/archive/marx/works/1881/ethnographical-notebooks/notebooks.pdf

[197] https://search.socialhistory.org/Record/ARCH00860

[198] https://www.marxists.org/archive/marx/works/cw/index.htm

[199] https://alexanderstreet.com/products/social-theory

[200] https://alexanderstreet-com.simsrad.net.ocs.mq.edu.au/page/history-imprints

[201] https://www.bbc.co.uk/programmes/p003k9jg

[202] http://purl.org/pressemappe20/folder/pe/011971

[203] https://web.archive.org/web/20110805112206/http://www.counterpunch.org/roberts10072009.html

[204] http://www.wsws.org/articles/2006/may2006/rock-m02.shtml

[205] http://chronicle.com/article/In-Praise-of-Marx/127027

[206] http://www.timesonline.co.uk/tol/news/politics/article4981065.ece

[207] http://www.marxists.org/archive/mandel/19xx/marx/

[208] https://web.archive.org/web/20120214101824/http://www.cato.org/pubs/journal/cj11n3/cj11n3-6.pdf

[209] http://www.emis.ams.org/journals/DMJDMV/xvol-icm/19/Dauben.MAN.html

[210] http://www.isj.org.uk/index.php4?id=486&issue=120

[211] http://marxmyths.org/

[212] http://www.iisg.nl/collections/marx/

[213] http://www.runmuki.com/paul/writing/marx.html

[214] http://www.econlib.org/library/Enc/bios/Marx.html

[215] http://business.time.com/2013/03/25/marxs-revenge-how-class-struggle-is-shaping-the-world/

[216] https://www.rollingstone.com/music/news/marx-was-right-five-surprising-ways-karl-marx-predicted-2014-20140130

[217] http://www.truthdig.com/report/item/karl_marx_was_right_20150531

[218] "Utopian Socialists" https://web.archive.org/web/20040214153800/http://cepa.newschool.edu/het/schools/utopia.htm.

[219] "Ricardian" http://cepa.newschool.edu/het/schools/ricardian.htm.

[220] *The essential Marx: the non-economic writings, a selection* (1979), New American Library, p. 359

[221] Saul K. Padover, Karl Marx (1977), On history and people, McGraw-Hill, p. 171

[222] Edward Staski, Jonathan B. Marks. 1992. *Evolutionary anthropology: an introduction to physical anthropology and archaeology*, Harcourt Brace Jovanovich College Publishers, p. 96

[223] John Bellamy Foster (2000), Marx's Ecology: Materialism and Nature, p. 197.

[224] "Marx to Ferdinand Lassalle in Berlin" http://www.marxists.org/archive/marx/works/1861/letters/61_01_16.htm.

[225] Karl Marx, Saul Kussiel Padover (1979), The letters of Karl Marx, Prentice-Hall, p. 157.

[226] Lane, David (2009), " Complexity Perspectives in Innovation and Social Change https://books.google.com/books?id=8KDdodrTBI8C&hl=es&source=gbs_navlinks_s" (2009), Springer, p. 122

[227] Institut Marksizma-Leninizma (1968), *Reminiscences of Marx and Engels*, Foreign Languages Publishing House, p. 106

[228] Richard Weikart (1999), "Socialist Darwinism: evolution in German socialist thought from Marx to Bernstein", International Scholars Publications, p 18

[229] Conway Zirkle (1959), "Evolution, Marxian Biology, and the Social Scene", University of Pennsylvania Press. p. 91

[230] The essential Marx: the non-economic writings, a selection, New American Library, 1979, p. 361

[231] John Spargo (1910), Karl Marx: His Life and Work, B.W. Huebsch, p. 200

[232] Stanley Edgar Hyman (1974), The tangled bank: Darwin, Marx, Frazer and Freud as imaginative writers, Atheneum, p. 121

[233] I. Bernard Cohen (1985), Revolution in Science, Harvard University Press, p. 345

[234] (1981),William F. O'Neill, "Educational Ideologies: Contemporary Expressions of Educational Philosophy", Goodyear Publishing Company, p. 74

[235] William F. O'Neill (1983), "Rethinking education: selected readings in the educational ideologies", Kendall/Hunt Pub. Co., p. 18

[236] Carter, Richard. "Marx of Respect" http://www.gruts.com/darwin/articles/2000/marx/index.htm (2000).

[237] Howard E. Gruber, Charles Darwin, Paul H. Barrett (1974), *Darwin on man: a psychological study of scientific creativity*, Wildwood House, p. 72

[238] Heinrich Lüssy (1995), Die Krise der Neuzeit, oder, Das Drama der prometheischen Selbstsetzung, Beerenverlag, p. 902

[239] John Bellamy Foster, Marx's Ecology: Materialism and Nature, p. 207.

[240] Paul Heyer, Nature, human nature, and society: Marx, Darwin, biology, and the human sciences (1982), Greenwood Press, p. 13

[241] Vucinich, Alexander. Darwin in Russian Thought http://publishing.cdlib.org/ucpressebooks/view?docId=ft5290063h;chunk.id=0;doc.view=print. Berkeley: University of California Press, c. 1988.

[242] //en.wikipedia.org/w/index.php?title=Template:Marxism&action=edit

[243] See in particular Chapter Two

[244] https://www.marxists.org/archive/marx/works/1848/communist-manifesto/ch02.htm, a process sometimes called "reification".

[245] Norman Geras, quoting Marx in his *Marx and Human Nature* (1983, p. 72)

[246] First chapter of the *1844 Manuscripts*

[247] https://www.marxists.org/archive/marx/works/1844/james-mill/index.htm

[248] https://www.marxists.org/archive/marx/works/1844/manuscripts/labour.htm

[249] https://www.marxists.org/archive/kamenka/1962/ethical-foundations/index.htm

[250] https://www.marxists.org/archive/meszaros/works/alien/

[251] http://www.nyu.edu/projects/ollman/books/a.php

[252] http://www.stanford.edu/~allenw/webpapers/Marxpreface.pdf

[253] https://books.google.com/books?id=1EGb3bRY2dIC

[254] https://books.google.com/books?id=5zDtOu1z9fAC

[255] Mike Beggs, "Zombie Marx and Modern Economics, or How I Learned to Stop Worrying and Forget the Transformation Problem." *Journal of Australian Political Economy*, issue 70, Summer 2012/13, p. 16 http://australianpe.wix.com/japehome#!current/c1cok; Gary Mongiovi, "Vulgar economy in Marxian garb: a critique of Temporal Single System Marxism." In: *Review of Radical Political Economics*, Vol. 34, Issue 4, December 2002, pp. 393-416, at p. 398.

[256] It is now interpreted that Ricardo's theory of value is not the labor theory of value, but the cost of production theory of value. See David Ricardo#Value theory

[257] e.g. see - Junankar, P. N., *Marx's economics*, Oxford : Philip Allan, 1982, or Peach, Terry "Interpreting Ricardo", Cambridge: Cambridge University Press, 1993,

[258] Ricardo, David (1823), 'Absolute Value and Exchange Value', in "The Works and Correspondence of David Ricardo", Volume 4, Cambridge University Press, 1951 and Sraffa, Piero and Maurice Dobb (1951), 'Introduction', in "The Works and Correspondence of David Ricardo", Volume 1, Cambridge University Press, 1951.

[259] Proudhon, Pierre J., 1851, *General Idea of the Revolution in the 19th Century*, study 6.

[260] Unless otherwise noted, the description of the labor process and the role of the value of means of production in this section are drawn from chapter 7 of *Capital* vol1 .

[261] In the case of instruments of labor, such as the roaster and the brewer (or even a ceramic cup) the value transferred to the cup of coffee is only a depreciated value calculated over the life of those instruments of labor according to some accounting convention.

[262] Marx, Capital, vol.1, p.

[263] Marx, Karl (1865). Value, Price and Profit. http://www.marxists.org/archive/marx/works/1865/value-price-profit/ch02.htm#c6

[264] Piero Sraffa and Maurice H. Dobb (1951). "General Preface", *The Works and Correspondence of David Ricardo*, Vol. 1, Cambridge University Press

[265] *Smith On Labour Value* http://www.ehu.es/kormazabal/SmithOnLaborValue.pdf

[266] Marx, Karl Value Price and Profit http://www.marxists.org/archive/marx/works/1865/value-price-profit/ch02.htm#c6

[267] Parrington vol 1 ch 3 http://xroads.virginia.edu/~Hyper/Parrington/vol1/bk02_01_ch03.html

[268] Karl Marx,*Value, Price and Profit*, 1865, Part VI.

[269] Ormazabal, Kepa M. (2006); Adam Smith on Labor and Value: Challenging the Standard Interpretation http://www.fae1-eao1.ehu.es/s0043-con/en/contenidos/informacion/00043_documentostrabajo/es_00043_do/adjuntos/il2006-26.pdf

[270] , New School University

[271] , History of Economic Thought, New School University

[272] Smith quoted in Whitaker, Albert C. *History and Criticism of the Labor Theory of Value http://socserv2.socsci.mcmaster.ca/~econ/ugcm/3ll3/whitaker/labortheory.pdf*, pp. 15–16

[273] Whitaker, Albert C. *History and Criticism of the Labor Theory of Value http://socserv2.socsci.mcmaster.ca/~econ/ugcm/3ll3/whitaker/labortheory.pdf*, pp. 15–16

[274] Fernando Vianello, (1990) "The Labour Theory of Value", Eatwell J., Milgate M., Newman P. (eds) in *Marxian Economics*, The New Palgrave, pp.233-246.

[275] Whitaker, Albert C. Albert C. Whitaker, History and Criticism of the Labor Theory of Value

[276] Jstor.org https://www.jstor.org/stable/1816138 King, Peter and Ripstein Arthur. Did Marx Hold a Labor Theory of Value?

[277] University of Toronto.ca http://individual.utoronto.ca/pking/unpublished/LTV.pdf

[278] Canterbery, E. Ray, *A Brief History of Economics: Artful Approaches to the Dismal Science, World Scientific (2001), pp. 52–53*

[279] "Thus, the classical solution of expressing the value of goods and services in terms of man hours, which was developed by the orthodox (political) economists of the time, was adopted by both Proudhon and Marx." http://www.inclusivedemocracy.org/dn/vol6/takis_proudhon.htm "Beyond Marx and Proudhon" by Takis Fotopoulos

[280] "The most basic difference is that the individualist anarchists rooted their ideas in the labour theory of value while the "anarcho"-capitalists favour mainstream marginalist theory." An Anarchist FAQ http://www.infoshop.org/page/AnarchistFAQSectionG1

[281] "Like Proudhon, they desired a (libertarian) socialist system based on the market but without exploitation and which rested on possession rather than capitalist private property" [[An Anarchist FAQ http://www.infoshop.org/page/AnarchistFAQSectionG1]]

[282] Palmer, Brian (2010-12-29) What do anarchists want from us? http://www.slate.com/id/2279457/, Slate.com

[283] Riggenbach, Jeff (2011-02-25) Josiah Warren: The First American Anarchist https://mises.org/daily/5067/Josiah-Warren-The-First-American-Anarchist, Mises Institute

[284] William Bailie, Josiah Warren: The First American Anarchist — A Sociological Study, Boston: Small, Maynard & Co., 1906, p. 20

[285] In Equitable Commerce, Warren writes, "If a priest is required to get a soul out of purgatory, he sets his price according to the value which the relatives set upon his prayers, instead of their cost to the priest. This, again, is cannibalism. The same amount of labor equally disagreeable, with equal wear and tear, performed by his customers, would be a just remuneration

[286] Wendy McElroy, ' Individualist Anarchism vs. "Libertarianism" and Anarchocommunism http://flag.blackened.net/daver/anarchism/mcelroy1.html," in the New Libertarian, issue #12, October, 1984.

[287] Smith writes: "The real price of every thing, what every thing really costs to the man who wants to acquire it, is the toil and trouble of acquiring it." Note, also, the sense of "labor" meaning "suffering".

[288] Charles A. Madison. "Anarchism in the United States". Journal of the History of Ideas, Vol. 6, No. 1. (Jan., 1945), pp. 53

[289] Miller, David. 1987. "Mutualism." The Blackwell Encyclopedia of Political Thought. Blackwell Publishing. p. 11

[290] Tandy, Francis D., 1896, Voluntary Socialism, chapter 6, paragraph 15.

[291] //en.wikipedia.org/w/index.php?title=Template:Marxian_economics&action=edit

[292] cf E F Schumacher,Small is Beautiful, Pt 1, ch 1. MMike Beggs, "Zombie Marx and Modern Economics, or How I Learned to Stop Worrying and Forget the Transformation Problem." Journal of Australian Political Economy, issue 70, Summer 2012/13, p. 16 http://australianpe.wix.com/japehome#!current/c1cok; Gary Mongiovi, "Vulgar economy in Marxian garb: a critique of Temporal Single System Marxism." In: Review of Radical Political Economics, Vol. 34, Issue 4, December 2002, pp. 393-416, at p. 398.

[293] Critique of the Gotha Program http://www.marxists.org/archive/marx/works/1875/gotha/ch01.htm. ch. 1.

[294] " Value, Price and Profit http://www.marxists.org/archive/marx/works/1865/value-price-profit/ch02.htm#c6 ch 6

[295] For the difference between wage workers and working animals or slaves confer: John R. Bell: Capitalism and the Dialectic - The Uno-Sekine Approach to Marxian Political Economy, p. 45. London, Pluto Press 2009

[296] Böhm von Bawerk, "Karl Marx and the Close of His System" Karl Marx and the Close of His System

[297] Ekelund, Jr., Robert B. and Robert F. Hebert (1997, 4th ed), A History of Economic Theory and Method, pp. 239–241

[298] Confer: Weizsäcker, Carl Christian von (2010): A New Technical Progress Function (1962). German Economic Review 11/3 (first publication of an article written in 1962); Weizsäcker Carl Christian von, and Paul A. Samuelson (1971): A new labor theory of value for rational planning through use of the bourgeois profit rate. Proceedings of the National Academy of Sciences (facsimile) https://www.ncbi.nlm.nih.gov/pmc/articles/PMC389151/.

[299] Kevin A. Carson, Studies in Mutualist Political Economy http://www.mutualist.org/id112.html chs. 1–3

[300] Joan Robinson, "Economic Philosophy" p39

[301] Philip Pilkington. Marx, Hegel, The Labour Theory of Value and Human Desire http://fixingtheeconomists.wordpress.com/2013/08/13/marx-hegel-the-labour-theory-of-value-and-human-desire/.

[302] Anson Rabinbach, " The human motor: Energy, fatigue, and the origins of modernity https//books.google.com"

[303] Jean Baudrillard, " Pour une critique de l'économie politique du signe http://www.gumilla.org/biblioteca/bases/biblo/texto/COM19751_23-25.pdf"

[304] Alf Hornborg, " Ecological economics, Marxism, and technological progress: Some explorations of the conceptual foundations of theories of ecologically unequal exchange." http://www.sciencedirect.com/science/article/pii/S0921800914001669

[305] Joan Martinez-Alier et al. "Weak comparability of values as a foundation for ecological economics" http://www.sciencedirect.com/science/article/pii/S0921800997001201.

[306] http://www.mtholyoke.edu/~fmoseley/Dussel.pdf

[307] //doi.org/10.1080/089356901101241569

[308] http://www.arte-fact.org/ccfbdspf.html

[309] http://www.marxists.org/archive/marx/works/1880/soc-utop/

[310] http://eurodos.chez-alice.fr/docu/econ/hagendorf_labour_theory_of_value_42008.pdf

[311] http://ssrn.com/paper=1489383

[312] http://www.debunking-economics.com/Papers/Marx/Keen_Marx_Thesis.pdf

[313] http://www.marxists.org/archive/marx/works/1867-c1/

[314] http://www.ehu.es/kormazabal/SmithOnLaborValue.pdf

[315] http://xroads.virginia.edu/~Hyper/Parrington/vol1/bk02_01_ch03.html

[316] https://www.springer.com/physics/complexity/book/978-94-007-2095-4

[317] https://web.archive.org/web/20070927202615/http://www.adamsmith.org/smith/won-index.htm

[318] http://www.adamsmith.org/smith/won-index.htm

[319] http://plato.stanford.edu/entries/marx/#3

[320] //doi.org/10.1215/00182702-14-4-564

[321] Schriften von Karl Marx: "Das Minifest der Kommunistischen Partei" (1948) und "Das Kapital", ernster Band (1867) http://www.unesco.de/kommunikation/mow/mow-deutschland/kommunistisches-manifest.html (UNESCO)

[322] Louise Yeoman. " Helen McFarlane – the radical feminist admired by Karl Marx http://bbc.com/news/uk-scotland-20475989". BBC Scotland. 25 November 2012.

[323] *Marx/Engels Collected Works*, Volume 6, p. xxvi

[324] Osborne, Peter. 1998. "Remember the Future? The Communist Manifesto as Historical and Cultural Form" in Panitch, Leo and Colin Leys, Eds., *The Communist Manifesto Now: Socialist Register, 1998* London: Merlin Press, p. 170. Available online from the Socialist Register http://socialistregister.com/index.php/srv/issue/view/434#.Vk5TIXhvlFU archives. Retrieved November 2015.

[325] Raines, John (2002). "Introduction". *Marx on Religion* (Marx, Karl). Philadelphia: Temple University Press. p. 5.

[326] Harman, Chris (2010). "The Manifesto and the World of 1848". *The Communist Manifesto* (Marx, Karl and Engels, Friedrich). Bloomsbury, London: Bookmarks. p. 3.

[327] Callinicos, Alex (2010). "The Manifesto and the Crisis Today". *The Communist Manifesto* (Marx, Karl and Engels, Friedrich). Bloomsbury, London: Bookmarks. p. 8.

[328] Steger, Manfred B. *The Quest for Evolutionary Socialism: Eduard Bernstein And Social Democracy.* Cambridge, England, UK; New York City, USA: Cambridge University Press, 1997. pp. 236–37.

[329] Micheline R. Ishay. The History of Human Rights: From Ancient Times to the Globalization Era. Berkeley and Lose Angeles, California: University of California Press, 2008. p. 148.

[330] Michael Harrington. *Socialism: Past and Future.* Reprint edition of original published in 1989. New York City: Arcade Publishing, 2011. pp. 249–50.

[331] The [*sic!*] is that of Joseph Schumpeter; see .

[332] Derrida, Jacques. " What is Ideology? https://www.marxists.org/reference/subject/philosophy/works/fr/derrida2.htm" in *Specters of Marx, the state of the debt, the Work of Mourning, & the New International*, translated by Peggy Kamuf, Routledge 1994.

[333] Warren, Christopher N (2016). " Big Leagues: Specters of Milton and Republican International Justice between Shakespeare and Marx. https://dx.doi.org/10.17613/M6VW8W" *Humanity: An International Journal of Human Rights, Humanitarianism, and Development*, Vol. 7.

[334] Rose, Jonathan (2001). *The Intellectual Life of the British Working Classes* https://books. google.com/books/about/The_Intellectual_Life_of_the_British_Wor.html?id=3B-qbvQTYyEC. Pgs. 26, 36-37, 122-25, 187.

[335] Taylor, Antony (2002). "Shakespeare and Radicalism: The Uses and Abuses of Shakespeare in Nineteenth-Century Popular Politics." *Historical Journal 45*, no. 2. Pgs. 357-79.

[336] Marx, Karl (1844). "On the Jewish Question."

[337] Warren, Christopher N (2016). " Big Leagues: Specters of Milton and Republican International Justice between Shakespeare and Marx https://dx.doi.org/10.17613/M6VW8W." *Humanity: An International Journal of Human Rights, Humanitarianism, and Development*, Vol. 7. Pg. 372.

[338] //citeseerx.ist.psu.edu/viewdoc/summary?doi=10.1.1.673.9426

[339] //doi.org/10.1257/jep 12.4.151

[340] //www.jstor.org/stable/2646899

[341] //doi.org/10.1086/256806

[342] //www.jstor.org/stable/1826126

[343] https://www.marxists.org/archive/marx/works/download/pdf/Manifesto.pdf

[344] http://www.marxists.org/archive/marx/works/1848/communist-manifesto/index.htm

[345] http://ciml.250x.com/archive/marx_engels/me_languages.html

[346] http://reader.digitale-sammlungen.de/en/fs1/object/display/bsb10859626_00001.html

[347] https://librivox.org

[348] https://www.youtube com/watch?v=dAujsDBZByA

[349] http://spip.modkraft.dk/tidsskriftcentret/undersider/article/det-kommunistiske-manifest-in

[350] //en.wikipedia.org/w/index.php?title=Template:Marxian_economics&action=edit

[351] //en.wikipedia.org/w/index.php?title=Template:Marxism&action=edit

[352] Described in Duncan Foley and Gérard Duménil, 2008, "Marx's analysis of capitalist production," *The New Palgrave Dictionary of Economics*, 2nd Edition. Abstract. http://www.dictionaryofeconomics.com/article?id=pde2008_M000399&edition

[353] See Helmut Reichelt, quoted in: Kubota, Ken: *Die dialektische Darstellung des allgemeinen Begriffs des Kapitals im Lichte der Philosophie Hegels. Zur logischen Analyse der politischen Ökonomie unter besonderer Berücksichtigung Adornos und der Forschungsergebnisse von Rubin, Backhaus, Reichelt, Uno und Sekine*, in: Beiträge zur Marx-Engels-Forschung. Neue Folge 2009, pp. 199–224, here p. 199.

[354] Angus Maddison, *Phases of Capitalist Development*. Oxford, 1982. p. 256, note.

[355] Capital, Vol I, Chap I (p. 39 in the Progress Publishers, Moscow, edition).

[356] Schools http://www.open.ac.uk/socialsciences/hetecon/schools.htm. HETecon.com. Retrieved on: August 23, 2007.

[357] V. K. Dmitriev, 1974 (1898), *Economic Essays on Value, Competition and Utility*. Cambridge: Cambridge Univ. Press.

[358] Ladislaus von Bortkiewicz, 1952 (1906–1907), "Value and Price in the Marxian System", *International Economic Papers* 2, 5–60; Ladislaus von Bortkiewicz, 1984 (1907), "On the Correction of Marx's Fundamental Theoretical Construction in the Third Volume of *Capital*". In Eugen von Böhm-Bawerk 1984 (1896), *Karl Marx and the Close of his System*, Philadelphia: Orion Editions.

[359] M. C. Howard and J. E. King. (1992) A History of Marxian Economics: Volume II, 1929–1990, chapter 12, sect. III. Princeton, NJ: Princeton Univ. Press.

[360] M. C. Howard and J. E. King. (1992) A History of Marxian Economics: Volume II, 1929–1990, chapter 7, sects. II–IV. Princeton, NJ: Princeton Univ. Press.

[361] See M. C. Howard and J. E. King, 1992, *A History of Marxian Economics: Volume II, 1929–1990*. Princeton, NJ: Princeton Univ. Press.

[362] "Only one conclusion is possible, namely, that the Marxian method of transformation [of commodity values into prices of production] is logically unsatisfactory." Paul M. Sweezy, 1970 (1942), *The Theory of Capitalist Development*, p. 15. New York: Modern Reader Paperbacks.

[363] Nobuo Okishio, 1961, "Technical Changes and the Rate of Profit," *Kobe University Economic Review* 7, pp. 85–99.

[364] "[P]hysical quantities ... suffice to determine the rate of profit (and the associated prices of production) .... [I]t follows that value magnitudes are, at best, redundant in the determination of the rate of profit (and prices of production)." "Marx's value reasoning—hardly a peripheral aspect

of his work—must therefore be abandoned, in the interest of developing a coherent materialist theory of capitalism." Ian Steedman, 1977, *Marx after Sraffa*, pp. 202, 207. London: New Left Books.

[365] "[The falling-rate-of-profit] position is rebutted in Chapter 5 by a theorem which states that ... competitive innovations result in a rising rate of profit. There seems to be no hope for a theory of the falling rate of profit within the strict confines of the environment that Marx suggested as relevant." John Roemer, *Analytical Foundations of Marxian Economic Theory*, p. 12. Cambridge: Cambridge Univ. Press, 1981.

[366] "An Error II is an inconsistency, whose removal through development of the theory leaves the foundations of the theory intact. Now I believe that Marx left us with a few Errors II." David Laibman, "Rhetoric and Substance in Value Theory" in Alan Freeman, Andrew Kliman, and Julian Wells (eds.), *The New Value Controversy and the Foundations of Economics*, Cheltenham, UK: Edward Elgar, 2004, p. 17

[367] See Andrew Kliman, *Reclaiming Marx's "Capital": A Refutation of the Myth of Inconsistency*, esp. pp. 210–11.

[368] Andrew Kliman, *Reclaiming Marx's "Capital"*, Lanham, MD: Lexington Books, p. 208, emphases in original.

[369] Robert M. Solow, "The Wide, Wide World of Wealth, "*New York Times*, March 28, 1988, excerpt https://www.nytimes.com/1988/03/20/books/the-wide-wide-world-of-wealth.html?pagewanted=2&src=pm (from a review of *The New Palgrave: A Dictionary of Economics*, 1987).

[370] Baran, P. and Sweezy, P. (1966). *Monopoly Capital: An essay on the American economic and social order*, Monthly Review Press, New York

[371] Jonathan Nitzan and Shimshon Bichler. *Capital as power: a study of order and creorder https://books.google.com/books?id=-qRKIpvTO6IC&dq=*. Taylor & Francis, 2009, p. 50

[372] //doi.org/10.1057/978-1-349-95121-5_1135-1

[373] //doi.org/10.1057/978-1-349-95121-5_1001-1

[374] http://www.dictionaryofeconomics.com/article?id=pde2008_S000449&edition=current&q=marxian&topicid=&result_number=1

[375] http://www.dictionaryofeconomics.com/article?id=pde2008_R000004&edition=current&q=marxian&topicid=&result_number=9

[376] https://www.worldcat.org/oclc/489902822

[377] https://www.worldcat.org/oclc/873921143

[378] https://www.nytimes.com/1988/03/20/books/the-wide-wide-world-of-wealth.html?scp=1

[379] //www.worldcat.org/oclc/799965716

[380] https://web.archive.org/web/20080512083757/http://cepa.newschool.edu/het/schools/marxian.htm

[381] http://cepa.newschool.edu/het/schools/marxian.htm

[382] http://www.economicpolicyresearch.org/

[383] http://www.marxists.org/subject/economy/index.htm

[384] https://web.archive.org/web/20080429202643/http://cepa.newschool.edu/het/schools/neomarx.htm

[385] http://cepa.newschool.edu/het/schools/neomarx.htm

[386] http://eurodos.free.fr/mime

[387] http://www.valuetheory.org

[388] http://www.marxist.com/reformism-or-revolution-6.htm

[389] http://sites.google.com/site/theendofthemarket/

[390] http://homepage.newschool.edu/~het/schools/neomarx.htm

[391] http://monthlyreview.org/2015/04/01/if-youre-so-smart-why-arent-you-rich/

[392] //en.wikipedia.org/w/index.php?title=Template:Marxism&action=edit

[393] Bridget O'Laughlin (1975) *Marxist Approaches in Anthropology* Annual Review of Anthropology Vol. 4: pp. 341–70 (October 1975) .
William Roseberry (1997) *Marx and Anthropology* Annual Review of Anthropology, Vol. 26: pp. 25–46 (October 1997)

[394] S. L. Becker (1984) "Marxist Approaches to Media Studies: The British Experience", Critical Studies in Mass Communication, 1(1): pp. 66–80.

[395] See Manuel Alvarado, Robin Gutch, and Tana Wollen (1987) *Learning the Media: Introduction to Media Teaching*, Palgrave Macmillan.

[396] Georges Haupt, Peter Fawcett, Eric Hobsbawm. *Aspects of International Socialism, 1871–1914: Essays by Georges Haupt*. Paperback Edition. Cambridge, England, UK: Cambridge University Press, 2010. pp. 18–19.

[397] Georges Haupt, Peter Fawcett, Eric Hobsbawm. *Aspects of International Socialism, 1871–1914: Essays by Georges Haupt*. Paperback Edition. Cambridge, England, UK: Cambridge University Press, 2010. pp. 12.

[398] *A Contribution to the Critique of Political Economy* (1859). Introduction.

[399] *Comparing Economic Systems in the Twenty-First Century* (2003) by Gregory and Stuart. p. 62. *Marx's Theory of Change*.

[400] Free will, non-predestination and non-determinism are emphasized in Marx's famous quote "Men make their own history". *The Eighteenth Brumaire of Louis Bonaparte* (1852).

[401] *Socialism, Utopian and Scientific* (1882). Chapter three.

[402] Lenin 1967 (1913). p. 15.

[403] Grundrisse: Foundations of the Critique of Political Economy, by Karl Marx & Martin Nicolaus, *Penguin Classics*, 1993, , p. 265

[404] Evans, p. 53; Marx's account of the theory is the Preface to *A Contribution to the Critique of Political Economy* (1859). http://www.marxists.org/archive/marx/works/1859/critique-pol-economy/index.htm. Another exposition of the theory is in *The German Ideology*. It, too, is available online from marxists.org http://www.marxists.org/archive/marx/works/1845/german-ideology.

[405] See *A Contribution to the Critique of Political Economy* (1859), Preface http://www.marxists.org/archive/marx/works/1859/critique-pol-economy/preface.htm, Progress Publishers, Moscow, 1977, with some notes by R. Rojas and Engels: *Anti-Dühring* (1877), Introduction General http://www.marxists.org/archive/marx/works/1877/anti-duhring/introduction.htm

[406] *The Communist Manifesto* (1847). Chapter one.

[407] Marx does not claim to have produced a master-key to history as historical materialism is not "an historico-philosophic theory of the *marche generale*, imposed by fate upon every people, whatever the historic circumstances in which it finds itself". Letter to editor of the Russian newspaper paper *Otetchestvennye Zapiskym* (1877). He explains that his ideas are based upon a concrete study of the actual conditions in Europe.

[408] Lenin 1967 (1913). p. 7.

[409] Marx 1849.

[410] "Alienation" entry, *A Dictionary of Sociology*

[411] Joseph McCarney: *Ideology and False Consciousness http://marxmyths.org/joseph-mccarney/article.htm*, April 2005

[412] Engels: Letter http://www.marxists.org/archive/marx/works/1893/letters/93_07_14.htm to Franz Mehring, (London 14 July 1893), Donna Torr, translator, in *Marx and Engels Correspondence*, International Publishers, 1968.

[413] Castro and Ramonet 2009. p. 100.

[414] "Withering Away of the State." In The Encyclopedia of Political Science, edited by George Thomas Kurian. Washington, DC: CQ Press, 2011. http://library.cqpress.com/teps/encyps_1775.1.

[415] Lenin 1967 (1913) p. 35–36.

[416] Samezo Kuruma (September 1929). "An Introduction to the Theory of Crisis." https://www.marxists.org/archive/kuruma/crisis-intro.htm At Marxists.org, trans. Michael Schauerte. Originally from the *Journal of the Ohara Institute for Social Research*, vol. 4, no. 1.

[417] "Accusing Guesde and Lafargue of 'revolutionary phrase-mongering' and of denying the value of reformist struggles, Marx made his famous remark that, if their politics represented Marxism, 'ce qu'il y a de certain c'est que moi, je ne suis pas Marxiste' ('what is certain is that I myself am not a Marxist')". See "Programme of the French Worker's Party" http://www.marxists.org/archive/marx/works/1880/05/parti-ouvrier.htm.

[418] Not found in search function at Draper Arkiv http://www.marxists.org/archive/draper/index.htm.

[419] Trigger 2007. pp. 326–40.

[420] Green 1981. p. 79.

[421] Allan G. Johnson, *The Blackwell dictionary of sociology: a user's guide to sociological language*, Wiley-Blackwell, 2000, , p. 183-84 (Google Books) https://books.google.com/books?id=V1kiW7x6J1MC&pg=PA183.

[422] "Marxist Sociology" http://www.bookrags.com/research/marxist-sociology-eos-03/, *Encyclopedia of Sociology*, Macmillan Reference, 2006.

[423] About the Section on Marxist Sociology http://www2.asanet.org/sectionmarxist/about.html

[424] Bottomore, T. B. 1983. A Dictionary of Marxist thought. Cambridge, Massachusetts: Harvard University Press.

[425] *The Communist Manifesto (1847). Chapter one.*

[426] See Coltman 2003 and Bourne 1986.

[427] Gianni Vattimo and Santiago Zabala. *Hermeneutic Communism: From Heidegger to Marx* Columbia University Press. 2011. p. 122

[428] M. C. Howard and J. E. King, 1992, *A History of Marxian Economics: Volume II, 1929–1990*. Princeton, NJ: Princeton Univ. Press.

[429] John Maynard Keynes. Essays in Persuasion. W. W. Norton & Company. 1991. p. 300

[430] Callinicos 2010. p. 12.

[431] For example,

[432] Held, David (1980), p. 16.

[433] M. C. Howard and J. E. King. (1992) A History of Marxian Economics: Volume II, 1929–1990, chapter 7, sects. II–IV. Princeton, NJ: Princeton Univ. Press.

[434] See M. C. Howard and J. E. King, 1992, *A History of Marxian Economics: Volume II, 1929–1990*. Princeton, NJ: Princeton Univ. Press.

[435] Kliman states that "Marx's value theory would be *necessarily wrong* if it were internally inconsistent. Internally inconsistent theories may be appealing, intuitively plausible and even obvious, and consistent with all available empirical evidence—but they cannot be right. It is necessary to reject them or correct them. Thus the alleged proofs of inconsistency trump all other considerations, disqualifying Marx's theory at the starting gate. By doing so, they provide the principal justification for the suppression of this theory as well as the suppression of, and the denial of resources needed to carry out, present-day research based upon it. This greatly inhibits its further development. So does the very charge of inconsistency. What person of intellectual integrity would want to join a research program founded on (what he believes to be) a theory that is internally inconsistent and therefore false?" (Andrew Kliman, *Reclaiming Marx's "Capital": A Refutation of the Myth of Inconsistency,* Lanham, MD: Lexington Books, 2007, p. 3, emphasis in original). However, in his book, Kliman presents an interpretation where these inconsistencies can be eliminated. The connection between the inconsistency allegations and the lack of study of Marx's theories was argued further by John Cassidy ("The Return of Karl Marx," *The New Yorker*, Oct. 20 & 27, 1997, p. 252): "His mathematical model of the economy, which depended on the idea that labor is the source of all value, was riven with internal inconsistencies and is rarely studied these days."

[436] Andrew Kliman, *Reclaiming Marx's "Capital"*, Lanham, MD: Lexington Books, p. 208, emphases in original.

[437] Herman Gorter, Anton Pannekoek, Sylvia Pankhurst, Otto Ruhl *Non-Leninist Marxism: Writings on the Workers Councils*. Red and Black, 2007.

[438] Ernesto Screpanti, Libertarian communism: Marx Engels and the Political Economy of Freedom, Palgrave Macmillan, London, 2007.

[439] Draper, Hal. "The Principle of Self-Emancipation in Marx and Engels" https://jps.library.utoronto.ca/index.php/srv/article/view/5333 *Socialist Register*. Vol 4.

[440] Chomsky, Noam. "Government In The Future" http://chomsky.info/audionvideo/19700216.mp3 Poetry Center of the New York YM-YWHA. Lecture.

[441] V. K. Dmitriev, 1974 (1898), *Economic Essays on Value, Competition and Utility*. Cambridge: Cambridge Univ. Press

[442] Ladislaus von Bortkiewicz, 1952 (1906–1907), "Value and Price in the Marxian System", *International Economic Papers* 2, 5–60; Ladislaus von Bortkiewicz, 1984 (1907), "On the Correction of Marx's Fundamental Theoretical Construction in the Third Volume of *Capital*".

In Eugen von Böhm-Bawerk 1984 (1896), *Karl Marx and the Close of his System*, Philadelphia: Orion Editions.

[443] M. C. Howard and J. E. King. (1992) A History of Marxian Economics: Volume II, 1929–1990, chapter 12, sect. III. Princeton, NJ: Princeton Univ. Press.

[444] Sennholz, Hans F. 'What We Can Know About The World" https://mises.org/daily/3910/What-We-Can-Know-About-the-World.

[445] Von Mises, Ludwig. "Omnipotent Government" https://books.google.com/books/about/Omnipotent_Government.html?id=QoOMaqfdpT4C.

[446] Gottfried Haberler in Milorad M. Drachkovitch (ed.), *Marxist Ideology in the Contemporary World – Its Appeals and Paradoxes* (New York: Praeger, 1966), p. 124.

[447] http://www.marxists.org/archive/lenin/works/1914/granat/index.htm

[448] http://www.marxists.org/archive/marx/works/1847/wage-labour/index.htm

[449] http://www.hawaii.edu/powerkills/NOTE12.HTM

[450] http://www.hawaii.edu/powerkills/CIP.CHAP5.HTM

[451] //tools.wmflabs.org/ftl/cgi-bin/ftl?st=wp&su=marxism

[452] //tools.wmflabs.org/ftl/cgi-bin/ftl?st=wp&su=marxism&library=0CHOOSE0

Article Sources and Contributors

The sources listed for each article provide more detailed licensing information including the copyright status, the copyright owner, and the license conditions.

Karl Marx *Source:* https://en.wikipedia.org/w/index.php?oldid=860401239 *License:* Creative Commons Attribution-Share Alike 3.0 *Contributors:* 72, A. Parrot, Abce2, Abelmoschus Esculentus, Ageispolis11, All Too Cynical, American In Brazil, Anime is a sin, Araceletorres, Arichard46, Arjayay, Aronlee90, AusLondonder, BeePee10, Bellerophon5685, Bonadea, Bongwarrior, Brennan medina, Britannicus, Byteflush, C.J. Griffin, CLCStudent, CSY Mary, Carlmarczisckool, Caroca2, Carrasco, Centurion of Rome, Chazza2443, Chazza2445, Chewings72, Citizen Canine, CloseLeech, ClueBot NG, Cocohead781, Ctbeiser, Cyberbot II, Dallwilson, Davide King, Donner60, Eddie891, Editor2020, Elekhh, Elias Is Mixed, F.DelDongo, FenixFeather, Free-KnowledgeCreator, Galobtter, Ghmyrtle, Gilliam, Hairy Dude, Haploidavey, Harrydickson11haddonroad, Haseeb, Helgi-S, Hmxhmx, Hsq7278, Iacobus, IntoThinAir, IronGargoyle, Ismail, Ivgnyl, Ixfd64, J 1982, JDuggan101, JackintheBox, James Joseph P. Smith, Jochen Burghardt, Johnpfmcguire, Jensey95, KJP1, Kaushwiki, Kelutral, Kencf0618, Kiillo, Kind Tennis Fan, LakesideMiners, Lamb27, Laszlo Panaflex, Leftwinguy92, Lil opioid, LilyKitty, Linkkerpar, Lionparty, Maczkopeti, MagicatthemovieS, Mandruss, Mark Zuccer, Master of Time, MasterOfHisOwnDomain, Max rspct, Mean as custard, Michaelhurwicz, Michihiro Yumoto Soga, MinnesotanUser, Montezuma II, Mramoeba, Muboshgu, Narky Blert, Nikkimaria, Non-dropframe, North Shoreman, Nosebagbear, Notreallymeeither, NottNott, Numbzoo, Nøkkenbuer, OZOO, Official Flynn, Ohnoitsjamie, Omnipaedista, Pablomartinez, Pezespe, Pgan002, Pharos, Pianpore888, Rachel0898, RainFall, Raritydash, RolandR, Samf4u, SaucyJimmy, SemiHypercube, Sessien, Shellwood, Simonm223, SkyGazer 512, Snowded, Steeliest, Straw Cat, Suandogg, Sugrammr, SvartMan, TheRealKarlMarx123, Tobby72, Tornado chaser, Ttocserp, UwuOSu-PAPA, Warshy, Wikiain, Wikiraven65, Wojsław Brożyna, Wrath X, Xx236, ZH8000, Zzuuzz, Алый Король, Гармонический Мир, Ватми, 149 anonymous edits 1

Influences on Karl Marx *Source:* https://en.wikipedia.org/w/index.php?oldid=859080153 *License:* Creative Commons Attribution-Share Alike 3.0 *Contributors:* Altair, Andysoh, Arges, Byelf2007, ClueBot NG, Crimson30, Dinosaur puppy, Edward, EnthusiastFR, Euchiasmus, Gilliam, Goethean, Goose friend, Hans Adler, InverseHypercube, Ira Leviton, Iridescent, JamesAM, Je Vous Ai Compris !!, Jeff5102, JenLouise, John of Reading, Khukri, Legotech, LilHelpa, Lugia2453, Marcuccitoy2, Matthew Fennell, MichaelGood, Omnipaedista, Pechenny, Qwertyus, Raffles mk, Rjwilmsi, RolandR, SchreiberBike, SheenShin, Sriharsh1234, Straw Cat, Tktktk, Ulric1313, Uppland, We66er, He A, 61 anonymous edits 47

Marx's theory of human nature *Source:* https://en.wikipedia.org/w/index.php?oldid=821566699 *License:* Creative Commons Attribution-Share Alike 3.0 *Contributors:* Anarchia, AnieHall, BD2412, Barticus88, Bender235, Bobo192, Breadandroses, Byelf2007, Charles Matthews, ChrisCork, ClueBot NG, Damifb, Dimadick, Edward, Ellis Runion, Erebus555, Esperant, Felix558, FreeKnowledgeCreator, Funandtrvl, Gentlecollapse6, Ginsuloft, Gregbard, GregorB, Gurch, Hashthug, Ian Pitchford, Ibrahim Husain Meraj, Ira Leviton, Iridescent, Jim1138, Jurriaan, Kazrak, Khazar2, Marek69, Materialscientist, Mild Bill Hiccup, Nathanian, Npepperell, Oliver Goransson, Omnipaedista, OsamaK, Rapsar, Rupert loup, Santa Sangre, SimmeD, StaceyLB1987, Superiority, Tempodivalse, The Vintage Feminist, Wilson44691, Гармонический Мир, 66 anonymous edits 59

Labor theory of value *Source:* https://en.wikipedia.org/w/index.php?oldid=858534998 *License:* Creative Commons Attribution-Share Alike 3.0 *Contributors:* 3298230932782302, A123214, Abc10, Agricola44, Al-Andalusi, Alex1011, Aliceinlampyland, Andkore, Andrew Lancaster, Andrey Andreev, Anthro-apology, Aps66, Artefactme, AvalerionV, BD2412, Banzai6666, Battlecry, Bender235, BillH76, Bobrayner, Byelf2007, Cambridge Optic, CarloMartinelli, Chris the speller, ChrisHutchinson, Chris Warren, Christophercolbert, ClueBot NG, Crito10, Cuati, DASonnenfeld, Don4of4, DoorsAjar, Eduen, Edward, Eurodos, Farjoun, Federico Tortorelli, Fengryffen, Fifelfoo, Frag-ail rock, Freshfroot, Fujo11, Gary, Gary123, George100, Gerrynobody, Goddun, GoingBatty, Gonji ha, Graham87, Gregbard, HandsomeMrToad, Hans Adler, Helvetius, Hendrick 99, Honglilai, I Feel Tired, Id4abel, Inkathi, Inswoon, Iridescent, JEN9841, JLMadrigal, Jack Upland, JesseRafe, Jim1111, Jonkerz, Jrtayloriv, Jurriaan, JzG, KCSARR, KG1138, Khazar, Kjbavaro, Kjk2.1, Kleuske, Knight1993, Koavf, Lalichii, LilHelpa, LittleWink, Lotje, Madliner, Magioladitis, Manticore, Mapet318, Marcocapelle, Me, Myself, and I are Here, Mean as custard, Mikcob, Misterparaphrastic, Moehrpi, Moooond, Mr Stephen, Mr pand, NawlinWiki, Nbarth, Nimzowitch, Noyster, Nøkkenbuer, Q5o7, Omnipaedista, Onel5969, Pbrooks, PerfectlyGoodInk, Peter Isotalo, Pgan002, Piero Testa, Piotrus, Plrk, ProKro, Qwerty12345, Rachel0898, Red Deathy, Redthoreau, Rich Farmbrough, Richardlord50, Rjwilmsi, RolandR, SA 13 Bro, Sdfahfajf, Seanc2017, Serois, Shellwood, Shevy11, Simon Peter Hughes, Somedifferentstuff, Squiver, Srich32977, Stellaring, Swagman2012, The Transhumanist, The Vintage Feminist, Theinstantmatrix, Toreightyone, Trentparsons, Ultimograph5, Velebam, Wadehagan12345, Wen D House, Wiae, Wikipelli, XxThePixelxX, YeOldeGentleman, Zzuuzz, 125 anonymous edits 71

The Communist Manifesto *Source:* https://en.wikipedia.org/w/index.php?oldid=860077629 *License:* Creative Commons Attribution-Share Alike 3.0 *Contributors:* AY KAY KASHHHHH, AusLondonder, Awesome editor, BDD, Bellerophon5685, Bkonrad, Bongwarrior, Boomer Vial, CAPTAIN RAJU, Carrite, Cbsdecker, Charles01, ClueBot NG, Commiep00, Comrade Penrose, Crystallizedcarbon, DVdm, Dagko, Damiens.rf, Danemark, Darchane Shines, Darylgolden, DavidLeighEllis, Davidboanuh, Dawnseeker2000, Dcirovic, DI2000, Dfiu28, Doprendek, Drewp123, Editorofthewiki, Esszet, Examplar, FreeKnowledgeCreator, Freshacconci, Gaius Cornelius, Gav Daddy262, Geckovsthesate, GeneralKutuzov, HafizHanif, Howcheng, IllaZilla, Indopug, Iron-Gargoyle, Itzreicool, J 1982, Jack Frost, Jdillonf, Jg2904, Jim1138, KNHaw, Kosack, LFdoR, Lacrimosus, Lbutterfield, Leutha, Lightlowemon, LilyKitty, LizardR8, Llightex, Luctor, Magyar25, MarnieV, Marianna251, Matamir, Mean as custard, MichealHunt69, Michipedian, MinnesotanUser, Mirogeorgiev1997, Mistbreeze, Number 57, Omnipaedista, Oshwah, Pablomartinez, Peter Leckey, Philip Trueman, PiyrStar93, PolicyReformer, PytilinskiE, Qzd, Raj stop, Ramaksoul2000, Reddishwagon, Rjwilmsi, RolandR, SA 13 Bro, Sdfahfajf, Seanc2017, Serois, Shellwood, Shevy11, Simon Peter Hughes, Somedifferentstuff, Squiver, Srich32977, Stellaring, Swagman2012, The Transhumanist, The Vintage Feminist, Theinstantmatrix, Toreightyone, Trentparsons, Ultimograph5, Velebam, Wadehagan12345, Wen D House, Wiae, Wikipelli, XxThePixelxX, YeOldeGentleman, Zzuuzz, 125 anonymous edits 87

Marxian economics *Source:* https://en.wikipedia.org/w/index.php?oldid=860504078 *License:* Creative Commons Attribution-Share Alike 3.0 *Contributors:* A8UDI, ACSE, Adair2324, AgambensreMarx, Aleksd, Amerul, Anarchangel, Aram33~enwiki, ArglebargleIV, Avoided, BD2412, Battlecry, Bear-rings, Bender235, Bkwillwm, Bobamnetriopsis, Bobrayner, Bronx Discount Liquor, Byelf2007, C.J. Griffin, Camw, Chendy, Chester Markel, Chris the speller, ClueBot NG, Correctionasdfg, Cuauti, Dawn Bard, Debresser, Dick Bos, Doprendek, Dthomsen8, Edward, EoGuy, Equilibrial, Eurodos, Everton, Fifelfoo, Financestudent, Flauius Claudius Iulianus, Flowerpotman, Fram, Frank, Frappyjohn, Frietjes, Fuddle, Gogolyea, Gonji ha, Gravuritas, Headbomb, Hexen hour, Hmains, I feel like a tourist, Inbloom2, Irishbrigade1942, Jamie7687, Jeepday, Jemappelleungarcon, Jim1138, John of Reading, JohnMaclean, Johndburger, Joseph Solis in Australia, Jrtayloriv, K4kant, Karl Wiki, Karmanatory, Khazar2, Kiefer.Wolfowitz, Knife-in-the-drawer, Koumz, Kuroze, LilyKitty, LudicrousTripe, Lycurgus, Magioladitis, Marcocapelle, Mark Ironie, Markypeepeeboys, Member, Michaelwuzthere, Michipedian, Mild Bill Hiccup, Miracle Pen, MrOllie, NawlinWiki, Nihiltres, Omnipaedista, Ontariodoy, PatientCompote, Petiatil, Prisencolin, Quebec99, Rationis, ReverendG, Richard Myers, Rigadoun, Rrburke, Rubentomas, Rupert loup, SherrySharnsi, Sindinero, Sjakkalle, Soap, Spylab, Srich32977, Sunray, Tbhotch, Tentinator, The Thing That Should Not Be, Theelkisinthekitchen, Thomasmeeks, Tom Morris, Trefork, Trilobitealive, YeOldeGentleman, Δ, Гармонический Мир, 168 anonymous edits 101

Marxism *Source:* https://en.wikipedia.org/w/index.php?oldid=860434593 *License:* Creative Commons Attribution-Share Alike 3.0 *Contributors:* 72, Abu Hajaar the first, Acroterion, Adfun12345, Alaudine, Alexandra IDV, Alfiejdavis01, Amortias, AntitheistAtheist1000, Aquillion, Artistology, Avalerion V, BITW01, Battlecry, C.Fred, CAPTAIN RAJU, CLCStudent, Charles Essie, Chevvin, Cloud2000, ClueBot NG, Collinsn, Cthomas3, Czar, Davide King, Derzzyn, Devonson4, Diannaa, Djharr2002, DonaldGump, Drewmutt, Drnitishkumar005, ERAMinc, Edderso, Editor2020, Eduen, Excirial, Favonian, Feniman228, Fugitron, Geckovsthesate, Gonchvsthesate, Gilliam, Gobonemud96, Helper201, Henry P. Smith, Home Lander, Hunner75, Ifnord, IronGargoyle, Iuhtboertgnvlejrhbtob, J 1982, JIMC89, JMJ1971, Jackfork, Jan sewi, Justanotherreader, JzG, Kawliga19, Kbog, Keynesian1234567890, Kjell Knudde, Kujilia, Larry Cole RBES, Lelaii, Llightex, Luis Goslin, Lukacris, Matthewglen, MendicantBias7, Mz7, NDPlume, Narky Blert, Nattycoh, Naturalhumandisasters, NewEnglandYankee, Newdictators, Nøkkenbuer, Omnipaedista, Oshwah, Ponyo, Quickfingers, Red-eyed demon, Redthoreau, Rich Farmbrough, Rob NorthMacbeth, Rupert loup, SUM1, Samf4u, Shellwood, Simo Hayha, Simplexity22, Socks253, Sol Pacificus, Spockofdagobah, Srich32977, Sroyalking, Stikkyy, Strongpoint, T-Esperantist93, Tony Fox, Tpbradbury, Tpwissaa, Travatar112, Velociraptor888, Vivek Ray, VoluntarySlave, Wallnot, Waltzzz, WereSpielChequers, What cat?, Wikiedit611, WikimaticImmunityB, William Avery, X1\, XYZiSpace, XenonNSMB, Yoshi24517, Zzuuzz, Ææ,lpokrmji, 150 anonymous edits 113

Image Sources, Licenses and Contributors

The sources listed for each image provide more detailed licensing information including the copyright status, the copyright owner, and the license conditions.

License

Index

www.ingramcontent.com/pod-product-compliance
Lightning Source LLC
Chambersburg PA
CBHW021145090426
42740CB00008B/947